A Persian Childhood

For Sedigh the Brave

A Persian Childhood

PARI COURTAULD

The Rubicon Press
57 Cornwall Gardens
London SW7 4BE

British Library Cataloguing in Publication Data

Courtauld, Pari
  A Persian childhood
  1. Iran. Social life, 1925-1979 - Biographies
  I. Title
  955.053092

ISBN 0-948695-19-6

Designed and typeset by The Rubicon Press
Printed and bound in Great Britain by Biddles Limited of Guildford and
    King's Lynn

Contents

Chapter 1

GOD

"Tell me a story," I asked Azra, the thin faced maiden.

"There *was* one," she began, "there was *not one*. Apart from God there was *no one*."

This prelude to all Persian stories started a chain of thought. Here was a good chance to resolve some doubts.

"Am I one?" I asked.

"Yes," she answered briefly.

"How long have I been?"

"Four years . . . I don't know. Five years."

I was glad I had been bold enough to ask. The grown-ups would have mocked me, but Azra was still young enough to be reliable. After all, how *was* one to know whether one was alive? There was little evidence. The meagre sensations I had experienced so far might have been a series of dreams. Dark rooms, many women chattering, a baby crying continuously - myself or not? Great heat in what was called Summer; stomach cramps. Did that suggest being alive?

This morning things were different. I had a feeling of well-being - of solidity. The spring sun was patting my back. The violets bordering the flower bed on which Azra and I were resting our feet gave out a delightful scent. I noticed for the first time the new shoots of the four magnificent weeping willows. Dancing about like green feathers, they were reflected in the round pond. Its water had just been changed and the gold fish were having a diving match.

"Doesn't God feel lonely being the *only* one?" I asked, breaking into a tangle of princesses, goblins and sleeping-draughts.

"Do you or do you not wish me to continue the story?" sighed Azra, peeved.

"Do as you please." But I had lost interest in the story. This business of being and not being was so fascinating. At the moment

1

everyone *was*, or so it seemed to me. Lots of children, parents, grandparents, servants, cousins by the dozen. My world was bursting at the seams with life.

There was no one in sight apart from an old gardener who was pottering about in a dug-in greenhouse taking out bedding plants a few at a time. His movements were slow and unobtrusive. Complete calm and peace were reigning the world as they do once or twice in one's life time.

"I suppose He is lonely," said Azra suddenly interrupting her story. "That is why He keeps creating more people."

Presently there was a commotion at the other end of the garden.

"Your mother's heathen visitor is leaving now. We had better get out of the way."

It was understood that one always had to hide or melt away at the approach of grown-ups except when one was cleaned up and shown off as a curiosity. I was not sure which I disliked most, being glared off or stared at. Life was an eternal apology for being.

We hid behind a hedge. Four ladies walked slowly towards the garden gate exchanging farewells. My mother and young cousin were dressed in the traditional Persian manner. Thin veils of pastel shades covered their hair and dresses. The third woman, whom I did not know, was dressed in the European style, and the 'heathen', a French lady, wore a pale costume and a white hat. They could not see us, so we crept behind the hedge and made our way to the scene of the morning's entertainment, a detached Russian-style house, called the guest-villa. Medina, a stout tribal woman, was already busy fumigating the drawing-room.

"I have taken the chair covers off; the china has gone to be scrubbed and I shall wash the infidel's footsteps from the carpet later."

"She didn't take off her shoes then?"

"No, thank goodness. It would have been much worse if she had."

"Shouldn't we be taking the sweetmeats back to the house?"

"No," was the emphatic answer. "These will not go back. They will be thrown away." Then she explained kindly so that the young girl should understand. "You see, dear, the infidel has touched these, and she being *najis* (untouchable), anything that she touches becomes *najis*."

Some inviting and delicious looking temptations were catching my eyes. Wrapped in shiny multicoloured paper, they were piled high on a silver dish. Without a word, I stretched out my hand and picked up two.

"You aren't going to eat those, my little one? Your mouth will become unclean."

It occurred to me, young as I was, that my mouth must already be unclean as I had been told that it was dirty to spit.

"But these were wrapped up. Nobody could have touched them," I protested.

"It's enough that the enemy of Islam should breathe on them."

The idea of that dignified foreign lady in the white hat breathing hard on a plate of chocolates, four feet away, was too much. I burst out laughing and put chocolate, paper and all, in my mouth.

"You can laugh, Miss, but remember, God will punish those who laugh at Him and His laws," said Medina in an awesome tone.

I was frightened. God seemed to get involved in everything.

Chapter 2

KING TO BE

Life was stylised and one's place in society was measured by the degree of homage one had to pay to others.

My mother paid a visit to my paternal grandmother every morning. Grandmother, Bishana, was a tiny woman nearing her hundredth birthday. As a girl, she had been smuggled inside an oversize Caucasian water melon through rebel territory. She insisted that two water melons made a good load for a camel. She had fine eyes and rosy cheeks and was quite invincible.

According to legend, she had "died" three times. On each occasion, as soon as the "corpse" was being arranged to face Mecca in accordance with Moslem practice, she had sneezed and sat up. On one occasion, noticing the mourners and the mullah reading holy verses at her side, she had exclaimed, "May I ask who is dying in this house?"

We listened with morbid interest; the story went that when this happened, water was being boiled for the final washing of the corpse. Everything was done at home in those days.

Going back to the routine, every morning my mother called on Granny, who was also her aunt (my parents being first cousins). This was a short visit. They exchanged greetings - no kissing except on New Year's Day, or after returning from a long journey. They asked after one another's health; then my mother would ask if her aunt had any special wishes for that day and gave her whatever part of the family news she considered might interest her (bad news was always suppressed).

Next came the Major, my father's nephew and right-hand man. He was granny's favourite grandson. He spent a little more time with her. He was charming and could not do enough for his relations.

The Major's visits to my mother were always accompanied by files, invoices, bills and any mail which had arrived at his office that day. He was in charge of paying the men-servants, paying taxes and supervising any building work that was in hand. In short, he took over the main organisation of the family in my father's absence. He also gave to my mother whatever political news he considered it was in her interest to know. My brothers Ismail and Jamshid were next in order of seniority, but they were such terrors that their visits were gladly dispensed with. As for my sisters and myself, we were not even fit to call, but were summoned to receive admonishment from some quarters and sweets from others. We were barely superior to the servants, had our meals with them in the early stages and slept where they chose to spread our bedding. Any one of them could scold us.

Suddenly, for no apparent reason, our position changed, and for a short time my sisters and I assumed star roles in the charade which followed. We were cleaned up, dressed in our best, put in a *droshky* drawn by two white horses and driven to the summer palace of the new dictator. The two women in charge kept on brain-

4

washing us from time to time: "Do not run; do not fight or shout; you must be on your best behaviour when we get there; do not disturb him. Remember - not only may he be our next king, but he has your destiny in his hands. Just be sweet and hand him the letter."

After we left the city gate and the moat behind, we drove for a while through an arid, stony desert, then gradually we passed villages with rough stone walls on top of which grew yellow flowers. Mohammad Beg, the driver, stopped; gave some water to the horses and some to us and then drove on. On the dusty road which ascended for five miles and ended at the foothills of the mighty Alborz mountains there was hardly any traffic. We overtook a sluggish army wagon. Later we saw a smart carriage travelling in the opposite direction. The last half mile or so was very rough and steep and the horses were breathing hard. We were there now and passed numberless sentries, eventually stopping in front of a white building. Our driver got down and after a long discussion with an officer, we were ushered to some seats under a shady tree where we sat awaiting the arrival of the great man.

It is very difficult to remember what happened next. My impression of the rest of that adventure is a gnawing hunger and my mother's great disappointment when, after our return, she heard of our failure to complete the mission. Apparently we had waited till four o'clock, but the object of our visit had not returned from the capital. Young Maryam had started to get troublesome, so it was decided that we should return.

After a great deal of hide-and-seek, we eventually succeeded on our third or fourth visit.

The final visit I remember clearly. We waited in the anteroom this time. It was a longish room and gave the impression of a passage. There was some good furniture about, but the chairs arranged against the wall were terribly hard. We waited interminably. Soldiers came and went. Eventually we were told that he was back and would see us presently. My baby sister was held back, but my elder sister and I were hurriedly pushed into the presence, the Letter foremost.

It was a large room and the French windows were open. In the middle of the room was standing a grey eyed giant in a familiar

5

military uniform. He gave the impression of having finished doing something very important - to his satisfaction. In short, he was in good humour. He told us kindly to sit down. My sister, thin and serious, shyly went forward and handed him Mama's letter. He bent down and chucked her under the chin. While he was opening the letter an orderly brought him a tray of food. There was bread, barbecued meat, pickles and a decanter of arak. He poured himself a small drink and drained it, then sat down to his meal while still reading the letter.

I could not keep my eyes off him. He was exceedingly handsome and the food he was eating smelt so good. I must have hypnotised him for suddenly he looked up and said, "Children, would you like some of this?" pointing to the roast meat. I must have been dribbling at the mouth at this point, but my junior status held me back. Our spokesman, my sister, said, "No, Sir, thank you."

The King-to-be dismissed us with kind words and a reassuring message to our mother.

Afterwards I was angry with Zari and asked why she would not let us accept food so good. She explained that "the man" drank and arak smelt nasty so she would not take food from him. Incidentally, it was not the only time I suffered as a result of her ultrasensitive nostrils.

Chapter 3

THE PRISONER

Noruz is a delightful festival. It celebrates nothing more formidable than the vernal equinox. Its institution is attributed to Jamshid, a legendary Persian king who also discovered wine. It is a very poor man who does not buy new clothes for his family at this festival, and it must be a destitute family who does not provide some sort of sweetmeat for visiting relations. And, thank God, it has nothing to do with religion - at least not with Islam. So when people give up thirteen days at the beginning of Spring to enjoyment, there is no guilt complex. I have often heard it said that Christmas, a religious festival, is an excuse for indulgence. *Noruz is* purely for indulgence to yourself and others. You repair broken friendships by a courtesy visit - a generous act few people are mean enough to ignore. You call on all your relations and visit bores and half-enemies. In fact, it is a renewal of your heart. You forgive and are forgiven.

On such a day my father was released from prison.

Our house had been spring-cleaned; the silver polished; sweetmeats and salted nuts prepared. The garden was tidied up. The paths were swept and sprinkled with water that brought up the divine scent of Persian earth. Children and servants, dressed in new clothes, darted to and fro, happy, not knowing why. Persian rugs were spread on the main paths, and on one sat my aged Grandmother, Bishana, in a white dress and veil, surrounded by her female relations.

Suddenly a stockily built manservant rushed rudely among the ladies asking for his *anam* (reward for bringing good news). "The master was on his way." This was followed by hushed silence. My father slowly walked in through the small gate which led from the *bironi* where he had been under house arrest. Dressed in a dark, fitted tunic and khaki trousers, he looked detached and rather sad. It was as though I were seeing him for the first time. He walked straight towards his mother and kissed her hand. She was weeping. Soon all the women were weeping and the children were beginning to snivel. It was more like a funeral than a reunion.

My mother, with her ever present sense of the occasion, put a small bundle wrapped in a white handkerchief in Papa's hand and whispered something. He plunged his hand into the bundle and scattered a handful of its contents in the air. A shower of tiny gold and silver coins, mixed with small white perfumed sweets called *noghle*, fell gleaming in a circle round him as he called, "Children come and collect your *aydi (Noruz* pressent)."

We rushed forward. The children and the maidservants went into a scrum cheered on by the grown-ups. In the excitement that followed, all sorrow was forgotten except by those whose fingers had been trodden upon. In a few moments the carpet was cleared of its glittering litter.

I opened two little hands and proudly displayed my booty of sweetmeats to Azra, who said, to my surprise, "You should have picked up the yellow ones."

7

Chapter 4

FATHER

Our father was a soldier. He came from a family of yeomen who were caught up in the Russo-Persian wars which raged for thirty years (1795-1828) in the region of their homeland, Southern Caucasia. Consequently, my father's forebears ended up as auxiliary soldiers.

After the final defeat at the hands of the Russians in 1828, and the loss of two Northern provinces, Erivan and Nakhejavan, these soldiers were given the alternative of embracing Christianity, if they wished to remain in their homes, or of going. A few hundred of them went. The Persian Government, ashamed of its inability to defend these provincials, offered them commissions in the Persian army and settled them, with their families, in the new North-West frontiers where their recent experiences and knowledge of the territory were useful. They were soon joined by others, and thus the *Mohajer*, or the émigré group, came into being. They banded together and helped each other's families who were in need. They had two things in common: love for their country and contempt for the central government.

When the crack Cossack regiment of the Persian army was formed, these men's sons, speaking Turkish and Russian, were ideal recruits. Thus, in due course, the émigrés became an influential military clique.

Not that there was anything "crack" about my grandfather, Mohebali Agha Mirpange, Brigadier Mohebali Agha. He was a tall, thin, ascetic man, with a pale face and a long black beard. (One of my profane cousins swore that he had heard him ridiculed on the stage as the "brainless brigadier".) Obviously he would have been more suited to the life of a cleric than of a soldier, except that he had no guile, no taste for luxuries, and no gift for intrigues - all

8

very necessary in those days for a holy man. How he came to marry a divorced bombshell like Bishana, no one knows.

Grandfather's religious leanings were directed at my father, who was prepared from an early age for a dedicated religious career. After he had finished his primary education, he was sent on numerous pilgrimages and eventually sent to study divinity at the theological college of Nejaf. His years at the seminary had the effect of turning him against religion. The greed, hypocrisy and sheer ignorance of his fellow clergy supplied him with a vast repertoire of anti-clerical stories. He was not to know that the class he gently mocked would, one day, make itself the object of comic relief for the rest of the world.

He was now an authorised *Mojtahed* or Islamic jurist and returned to Tehran where a marriage had been arranged between him and his beautiful fourteen year old cousin, Monavar. The bride said she liked him, but she would never marry an *akhund*. (*Akhund* and *mullah* are interchangeable names for Moslem clergy, but my father always used the term *akhund* for those of whom he disapproved.) Her own father was a Sardar and chief of military staff. A commission was quickly arranged for my father, and he appeared in a Cossack officer's uniform at his wedding. He never regretted his lost holiness.

Although the army was less devious than the mosque, pay was poor and officers had to be subsidised by their parents and were posted from station to station.

Papa was temperamentally suited to administrative work. He was often sent to tribal areas where the tribesmen were quarrelling among themselves or with their neighbours. His knowledge of Islamic law, by which the life of the country was then governed, gave him authority in the matter of land tenure and inheritance disputes. He liked disentangling problems. He also spoke Turkish, which is jokingly called the national language of Persian peasants, and thus he could talk to men directly.

His happiest time was his years among the Turkomans, the wild, independent tribes who lived on the plains of North-East Persia. These were a warlike people who bred fine horses, prized good guns, were utterly contemptuous of authority, and fought bloody battles among themselves. These skirmishes took them backwards and forwards across the Russo-Persian frontiers. They made such a nuisance of themselves that the two Governments agreed to set up a boundaries commission, with a Persian officer and a Russian commissar to attend to the cases of illegal infiltration, banditry, etc. In this capacity my father worked with satisfaction for many years. He got on well with the Russians, liked the commissars, and learnt to speak Russian moderately well. He also loved the unruly, sporting Turkomans, and delighted in dealing with them.

The following, much-told story has stuck in my memory. He once captured the leaders of two feuding families who were responsible for many murders and were determined to destroy one another. He had them chained securely to two posts ten yards apart in a barn. At first they tried to spit at each other and shouted abuse until they became hoarse. For the next few days they turned their backs on each other and kept silent. Each day the quality of their food was made worse until they began complaining mutually. When eventually their misery exceeded their venom and they began to speak to each other, Papa went to see them and offered himself as mediator. After a few days the matter was sorted out, but before the men were unchained, one promised to wed his daughter to his enemy's son. My father had them released. He had great respect for Turkoman manliness, for they never broke a promise.

My mother, however, maintained that Papa's satisfaction had other sources. He often spoke about the Russian Commissar's sister-in-law, who "had a lovely voice and whose red dress attracted the cattle". Whatever the truth, there is no doubt that a European girl would have had a field day among all those gallant men. There was no question of taking a wife to the wilds of the Turkoman Sahra. My mother stayed in Tehran with her in-laws and her family of five boys, while Papa worked in Eshgh-Abad, which translated into English literally means "Lovestead".

10

Chapter 5

THE HOUSE

At about this time, my grandparents bought their last house. This was a long, low building in the most northerly part of the capital, not yet fashionable, but quite cheap. One room deep and seven rooms long, all joined by double doors in a straight line, this was the most perfect course I have known for racing shoeless on Persian carpets.

The house was in the shape of a 'T'. Most of the living rooms were in the crossbar of the 'T', facing north with a view over the Alborz peaks. A wide balcony stretched along each wing of the south side terminating in two sets of steps leading down into two courtyards each having a small deep pond with goldfish. There were four dusty flower beds, some white jasmines, lilacs, pomegranates and apple trees. A series of vaulted basements ran under the rooms and were used for storage and a refuge from midsummer heat. The vertical stroke of the 'T' contained a room, two steps below the general level of the house, and an attic, connected in my memory with jam.

My mother lived in one part of the house, facing the slightly larger courtyard, and my grandparents lived in the other. From the corner of their courtyard a passage led into the kitchen quarters - a bleak, treeless yard lined on three sides by small rooms for the servants, and on the fourth by a long, black, smoky kitchen. In the pavement of this yard were small, brick-lined drain-holes called *chahak*, where children were allowed to make water, and women emptied their buckets and washtubs after laundry. It was a depressing place, where most of the domestic chores were done. Old women, wrapped in veils, sat for hours sorting out and cleaning rice in large copper trays. All the food was cooked here and taken separately to each household.

11

My grandmother, the mistress of the house, tried to establish good relations with her neighbours, who were mainly émigré and other military families. But her neighbours to the east were a rich and sophisticated merchant family who lived in an elegant house with a fine drawing-room decorated with mural paintings representing Armenian women in various romantic attitudes. They obviously didn't think much of their simple provincial neighbours. One day, as Bishana was talking to the merchant's wife, whose name was, appropriately, Tajerbashi (Merchant), the woman suddenly mentioned that an owl had been seen perched on their joint walls. She hastened to explain that this symbol of bad luck had had its head towards grandmother's house and only its harmless tail towards her own.

However, in this case, it turned out that the bird's tail was the unlucky end. Within six months Tajerbashi went bankrupt and had a stroke, and his family dispersed, selling his house and garden for a song.

At about this time, my mother's father, the Sardar, died, leaving her some money. She bought the merchant's house as an investment (it was later to be used as a *bironi*, or office) and had the waste land to the north of the house landscaped and an extraordinary bathhouse in the corner of the new garden built.

Chapter 6

THE LEADER

With the Great War raging in Europe, convulsions shaking the foundation of the Russian Empire, and the crumbling of the Ottoman Empire, prolonged tremors were beginning to be felt inside Persia which up to now had been an archaic, enclosed and untouched kingdom. Successive Persian Monarchs had made spectacular journeys to Europe and Russia and procured small loans which temporarily stopped the rickety structure from collapsing. But the weak

Persian economy could not be saved by a blood transfusion alone. The powerful tribes in the west and south were now in rebellion. The Army and Civil Servants could not be paid for months on end. Just as Wassmus, a famous German Agent, had set out earlier to foment the southern tribes, now a Bolshevik Agent called Mirza Kuchik Khan had set up his headquarters in the Mazandaran forests and was busy burning the prosperous Caspian cities. As for the British, they were behaving like assured masters, raising a Persian force and fighting here, there and everywhere in pursuit of their own aims. Meanwhile, the inoffensive and ineffectual little Ahmad Shah Ghajar who had inherited the Peacock Throne was completely impotent to deal with the ever increasing chaos.

My father, a brigadier in his forties, returned to the capital, to a predominantly male family. He was delighted, however, when after the prescribed period, my mother presented him with twin girls - my sisters Zari and Gohar.

He was then attached to the General Staff headquarters. About this time he met a brilliant young colonel, Reza Khan. A very attractive and original man, he had risen from the ranks, had been through numerous campaigns and was absolutely fearless. While most men were deploring the disappearance of the two Great Powers in the North, who had acted as a balance in Great Power politics, he was jubilant that the ogres had died, which increased Persia's chances of continuing as an independent country. And while everyone was wondering how the country was going to survive the next few months, Reza Khan believed fervently that Persians could and must save themselves, clear away the debris, and begin a new course of greatness. My father admired him as a child admires a bulldozer; he was resolute, unhesitant, ready to move mountains.

In the chaotic conditions which prevailed at that time, Reza Khan's military genius was very much in demand. It was a measure of the desperate condition of the country that in a thoroughly nepotic and corrupt administration, a man with no backing should be asked to lead its armies, solely on the basis of his own merit. He took his regiment with its émigré contingents on numerous campaigns and succeeded in all of them.

13

According to my mother, the first sound I heard when I leapt into this world was the whistling of bullets. During the night, while my mother was in labour, some sort of political struggle was going on around Tehran. At dawn, when I was being put into my mother's arms, a message came from my father saying "We have captured Tehran and I am safe". "We" were the Cossack Regiment of the Persian Army led by Reza Khan. But my mother did not see him for another two days.

I always loved this story and liked to pretend that the whole fireworks display was for my benefit.

However, this single coup changed things drastically. The Army was no longer a tool, but a force in its own right. Reza Khan soon became the head of the armed forces and most of his colleagues were promoted to positions of responsibility.

Chapter 7

ISFAHAN

The appointment to Isfahan was the highlight of my father's career. It was also the happiest time my family and their dependants experienced collectively.

Isfahan's legend and beauty, its incredible plenty, and the inhabitants' artistic vitality were forever stamped on the memory of everyone concerned.

It all began with the insurrection of the many clergy attached to the three great mosques, and the famous theological college. The insurrection, like many others of this period, was encouraged by the weakness of the Central Government. The *akhunds*, finding no effective opposition, claimed much public and some private land as *moghufé* or endowed property. They hired gunmen and local bandits to enforce their claims. The dispossessed landlords and local authorities bombarded the Prince Resident with petitions demanding justice. He asked Tehran for direction. A government

14

representative was sent out and was lynched on arrival. The authorities were alarmed and sent an urgent request for armed intervention.

My father, who was then Military Governor of Tehran, was hurriedly appointed the new governor of Isfahan and sent out at the head of a small detachment of soldiers.

The road from the capital to Isfahan was practically non-existent in those days and there was hardly any motor transport in the army. It took them nearly a week to get there. My father took the precaution of sending a couple of friendly mullahs in advance to make a reconnaisance. They came back and met him on the last lap of the journey reporting on the *akhunds'* strength and designs.

On the first night of my father's arrival in the city, soon after midnight, the attack came. The *akhunds*, carrying an assortment of knives, pistols and clubs, rushed upon the Governor's residence and stormed its doors and windows, but the soldiers who were waiting for them outside the building, behind the garden walls, fell upon them and took many prisoners. Another wave of *akhunds* rushed in and met the same fate.

At dawn my father went to inspect the prisoners and was aghast to see rows and rows of clean-shaven men chained together by their hands.

In a country where the length of a clergyman's beard was as good as a solid bank account, this nudity was unforgivable. My father's lively young assistant, Captain Atapur, took all the blame. He explained that, in his opinion "beard shed" was better than bloodshed, and pointed out that nothing short of mass murder would stop these chaps (in possession of their beards) from ascending the pulpit and making trouble in the immediate future. Papa saw the logic of this argument and asked what was to be done now. He replied, "We could send them on a long pilgrimage at the expense of the city". This was done and soon peace was restored. After six months my father sent for my mother and the rest of us to join him.

The move from Tehran to Isfahan became a favourite family saga and is still told with relish by an old nanny, the only surviving servant on that journey. My mother was accompanied by eight children, two nannies and three maids. They travelled in a Ford and a Studebaker, driven by two Armenian brothers. How on earth did they all get in?

In response to my father's request, a company of soldiers escorted the family as far as Delijan. The soldiers travelled in open horse-drawn wagons and the cars had to adjust their speed to them. It was the first time any of the family had travelled by motor car and they found the experience overwhelming. The journey, which now takes six hours to complete, took them four days and they marvelled at its speed and comfort. The old nanny used to say, "And he drove round the hairpin bend like the wind. We all held our breath and prayed to the Imams not send us to our deaths in the company of the Armenian infidel. But we dared not speak until one of the boys was sick and your mother bade the *shoefor* (chauffeur) to stop and told him that he must not drive so dangerously."

The *shoefor* must have been pretty nervous himself for he caught baby Maryam's swaddled feet in the car door. Everyone expected her feet to drop off, but the only casualty was her little toe-nail. At last they arrived at Delijan where father met them, sent back the soldiers, and accompanied them to Isfahan.

Still travelling through the bleak desert, they saw in the distance a green vista of gardens and orchards, a wide river spanned by magnificent bridges, and the shiny domes of the great mosques of Isfahan. They were overjoyed. It was like approaching paradise, and like paradise, it kept its promise of continued bliss.

They found life in Government House very pleasant: attention was lavished on them, even the servants received V.I.P. treatment. What they liked even better was the incredible plenty of the city. Heaps of excellent fruit and nougat were daily brought to the house and consumed by the children and the servants. They visited the bazaars and found it difficult to spend a *toman* in a single purchase. When they did, they were so overloaded that a coolie had to be hired.

My mother sent to Tehran for lengths of linen and engaged local women to embroider house linen with the delicate *cheshme-duzi* work of Isfahan. These tablecloths lasted my family for nearly half a century. Silver was dirt cheap. My mother commissioned craftsmen to make tea and coffee sets, trays and goblets with the

16

most charming designs. The Governor's salary of twelve thousand *tomans*, tax free, was, in those days colossal by Persian standards, but Papa worked hard for it. He now set up special courts to deal with claims arising out of the *akhunds'* actions.

One day an unknown little mullah in an *aba* and black turban came to see him. Father asked him what he wanted and the man replied that he wanted his beard shaved. The conversation that followed was something like this:

Father: If this is your idea of a joke, please note that I am very busy and not a barber.
Mullah: But with respect you are a barber and a very kind one.
Father (angry): Would you make yourself clear?
Mullah: Well, it is like this: nine months ago I was poor, out of work and in debt. A misguided fellow *akhund* suggested that if I helped to raid the Government House and rout its new tenant, I could share in the loot. So I joined the mob that attacked you on your first night here. I was caught, given a hard beating, which I admit I deserved, then my beard was shaved off. The next day I was given two hundred *tomans* compensation for my beard and exiled to Mashed. Now, I always wanted to go on a pilgrimage to that lovely shrine, but never before had the means to. I stayed three months in that holy city until my beard grew nice and thick, then I returned to Isfahan. I paid off my old debt which amounted to fifty *tomans*, married off my daughter and got a wife for my son. Now I am here to thank you for enabling me to do all this and to put my new beard at your disposal.

After order was restored to Isfahan and Shiraz, which was simultaneously governed by my father's good friend General Mahmud Khan Irom, it was announced that the monarch would visit the southern regions. This visit was accompanied by all the pomp and ceremonial attached to the movement of the Imperial Court since time immemorial. Numerous ministers, courtiers and functionaries travelled with His Imperial Majesty Ahmad Shah Ghajar. Yet in the photographs taken at the time the only person standing out from the group is Reza Khan. He towers above the five-foot-

17

nothing of the monarch and obliterates him.

'Chélél Sotun' (the palace of forty pillars which, in fact, has only twenty), the residence of the Shah's relative Sarem-e-Douleh, was chosen to accommodate His Majesty, and the local dignitaries were honoured to act host to the courtiers. There were no ladies in the party.

Isfahan was overjoyed with this undeserved honour. Banquets were given, fireworks sent up and there was a general atmosphere of festivity.

My mother had a great deal of extra work at this time connected with the visit, the most important being the banquet at Government House in honour of the Royal Party. She had to organise dinner for three hundred people in four *talars* (long reception rooms).

The custom then was to have the meal in relays. A long *sofreh* (oil cloth) was spread on the carpet and covered by a *ghalamkar* or hand-printed cotton cloth. On this, sweet and savoury dishes were laid at intervals to make a charming pattern; also to allow for easy reach. On each side, such plates and cutlery that could be found were laid out. Pickles and sweetmeats were there, as well as iced sherbets and glasses. Fruit was piled up on high dishes and melons cubed in their skins. Space was allowed for the hot dishes which were brought in immediately before dinner was served. The monarch, or the most honoured guest, would sit at the top of the *sofreh* on the cushioned floor, getting naturally the best china and silver and many servants behind to see to his needs. He was flanked by ministers and courtiers in order of their rank. Whilst there was a great deal of *taarof* (courtesy in the offering of advantage and precedence to others), a sharp eye was kept on the maintenance of one's place in both directions. Whereas few people had to be literally put in their places, many over-modest celebrities had to be physically hauled from near the door to the top of the room (every room had, of course, a top). The guests never sat down until asked by their host to do so.

Each guest kept the same plate throughout the meal and helped himself and his neighbours to whatever was fancied. There was no order of dishes. Speeches were not made during the meal, but neighbours and groups chatted and laughed. The noise pro-

18

duced by this was generally much louder at the top than at the bottom of the room. After dinner was over, decorated brass water jugs and basins were brought in for dirty hands to be washed. Then the guests left the room, the servants cleared the *sofreh*, laid clean china and cutlery, and the secondary guests were fed with the same menu, minus a few choice dishes.

After this came the turn of the servants, who also behaved with formal courtesy towards one another. This arrangement also applied to the harem (women's quarters). After everyone had eaten, whatever was left of the food was distributed among the numerous beggars who never failed to turn up at the back door wherever there was a banquet; as did the dogs, who gathered to pick the bones.

Some of us who have experienced modern Persian receptions cannot fail to regret the passing of such an orderly and dignified procedure. The absence of women and alcoholic beverages at meals concentrated the mind entirely on food, so that most men were 'gourmets' and had very sensitive palates.

To come back to our banquet, although my mother organised the feeding of three hundred people she, according to etiquette, could not be seen even by her royal guest. Her only part in it was to supervise the smooth running of the feast and the excellence of the dinner.

Just before the *talar* doors were thrown open to the guests, she, with her women, looked in to see that everything was in order. They inspected the piles of steaming, saffroned rice, barbecued lamb kept warm in flat bread, and they put fresh ice in the sherbets. Suddenly, a black cat rushed in from nowhere, raced through the pickles and sweets, stepping into the pilau and scattered rice. It then picked up a whole chicken in its mouth and disappeared through a side door. The women nearly had fits. What with the mess in the *sofreh* and the imminent entry of the King into the *talar*, a message was quickly sent to the master of ceremonies to hold up the party for a few minutes. The black cat was, of course, never seen again.

19

The Isfahan year had the atmosphere of a joyful and carefree holiday, or a long picnic on a spring day. The maids remembered with such pleasure the day they were sent to the bazaars to buy themselves golden earrings and bracelets - the story of that day filled many of my dark childhood nights later. And, oh! how we laughed when old Fatemeh recalled the loud knock on the garden gate early one morning. She rushed to open it anticipating some emergency, when a serious but foul-looking character asked her politely whether she had any *keke* to spare. Dumbfounded, she thought the man was either a libertine or mad, and chased him halfway down the road. It turned out that he was a *bona fide* market gardener on his daily search for human manure to nourish his melons with.

Alas, from all this great feast, all my young memory could retain was hiding from a long-horned deer under a blanket in an orchard and watching my mother in a white summer dress pack silver in a wooden box.

Chapter 8

THE TWINS

The twins were not identical. In fact, they did not have much in common apart from their sex. One was fat, healthy and beautiful and was named Gohar or Gem; the other, small, whining and irritable, was not expected to live. She was called Zari. She refused to take her mother's breast. A wet nurse was hurriedly found for her: she sucked once and was sick. In despair, they called the doctor. He said human milk was too rich, perhaps cow's milk would suit her better. Not better? Perhaps it ought to be diluted. Obviously, the child had a weak digestive system. A cow was bought and an enclosure made for it at the end of the garden. The child survived - but only just. She put on hardly any weight and sometimes would not eat for days on end. The household was in despair as she was the special pet of her grandparents as well as her parents. The child

20

exploited her weakness ruthlessly. On one occasion, when she was suffering from some infant complaint, she refused to take medicine. No amount of persuasion or bribes would induce her to take the nasty stuff. Someone had a brilliant idea. The nanny cow was brought to her window, all draped in pink brocade. She laughed and took the medicine.

Everyone sighed and wondered why she couldn't be like her twin sister who was chubby, pink-cheeked and no trouble at all. Gohar had hardly had any illness to speak of except for a touch of malaria, and was receiving treatment for this. Every day the wet nurse, who had stayed on as nanny, walked with her to the nearby surgery of an elderly and much respected doctor. The first time he amused the child by showing her the spirit lamp, lighting it and sterilising the instruments in front of her. But, as soon as she experienced the needle, she screamed. Didn't like it at all. She did this every time now. The nurse excused her, saying "She is timid. Doesn't mind swallowing medicine, but hates being hurt."

To spare the child unnecessary distress, on this particular day the doctor made all his preparations in the next room and quietly injected her bare thigh while she was sucking her thumb in nanny's arms. She gave a long scream and by the time he had finished rubbing alcohol on the jab she was dead.

Chapter 9

THE TIGER

Our father was recalled to the capital and appointed to the Cabinet. In the last three years honours had been heaped upon him. He was a general and Ahmad Shah had bestowed upon him the title of Amir-Eghtedar (Iktidar, Foreign Office Archives). His three eldest sons had been whisked off by the Army and sent to military schools in France for their education, a privilege available to a very few Persians at that time.

As with all ministerial households, the family found itself in possession of a great number of friends. To cope with the entertainment of the invited and the uninvited visitors, a new villa was built on the north-west side of the garden. It was a modern, white building of six rooms, a delicate wisteria covered terrace, and some vaulted basements used as orangeries in winter and living quarters in summer. Soon it was necessary to build stables and a garage.

Parkinson's law immediately applied. The villa was never free of guests while my father was in office. The office was now the Ministry of Communication and later the Ministry of Home Affairs. During this latter period, the pressure on the villa was greatest of all. Persians sensibly do not believe in conducting their affairs through correspondence with a faceless respondent. The most popular method of access was to find someone who had the slightest claim of kinship or friendship with the man in power. Once you had got your letter of introduction, the man was at your mercy until your aim was achieved. Guests arrived from far-off cities such as Hamadan and Tabriz, by themselves or with their families. It was against the rules of hospitality to turn them away and once they settled down it was impossible to turn them out except by inviting other guests who would create congestion and make it too uncomfortable for the longer-staying guests. Thus, the Persian saying "guests do not like guests - hosts do not like any of them".

The most memorable guest was my father's old friend Amir-Afshar, the wealthy Khan of the Afshar tribes in the North-West. He wrote that he was coming to Tehran to seek concessions for his tribe and would stay at our house. The villa was made ready and my family prepared to receive him with his few companions. One evening he arrived on horseback with a bodyguard of forty horsemen. Our little road suddenly became choked with dusty and wild-looking moustachioed men on horses. My father welcomed his friend, a frail and civilised gentleman, and after the usual greetings, suggested that he could perhaps allow his men and horses to be billeted in the nearby barracks, as obviously there was not enough room for such a crowd. There was a long whispered conversation and the answer was: the horses could go, but the men would certainly not leave the body they were supposed to be guarding.

"But where would they all sleep?"

"Oh, that didn't matter. They could sleep on the floor using their sheepskin greatcoats as cover. You must not worry about this riff-raff."

22

There was no point in arguing and one must not appear to be inhospitable. Masses of food was prepared that night and twice daily for the next five weeks. Huge copper trays went into the villa loaded with rice and meat with no end of loaves. The men sat round the trays dipping their fingers into them. What a jolly lot of men they must have been!

My mother's bathhouse was opposite the villa. She asked for it to be heated and got ready, but was told that she couldn't use it as men were sleeping on the changing-room platform. This made her very angry. She put pressure on my father to hasten the matter of the tribe's affairs and release her precious bathhouse.

After five weeks the guests left in high spirits. The Khan presented my father with an excellent Arab horse. When the women went in to clean the villa, they found the place crawling with lice, and carpets and upholstery stained with food and grease. What really shocked them was the condition of the bathhouse which had been used as a communal latrine. Mama was utterly dismayed. She insisted that every single tile on the floor and walls of the *hammam* be replaced and the place completely redecorated. It was three months before the bath could be used again.

I sometimes try to imagine my mother's mounting frustration with the rise of the family fortunes. It was bad enough to be beautiful, intelligent and responsible for the well-being of so many people as well as being anonymous, self-effacing and almost invisible. Now, to make matters worse, she hardly saw anything of her husband, for my father attended to his work all day only snatching a few minutes for lunch at home, which was usually disturbed by petitioners. In the evening he had to go to parties, official and unofficial, always with the same friends - Reza Khan, Sardar Assad, the Bakhtiari Chief, Taymour-Tash, and many other top brass and smart aristocrats. This was the group on which all eyes were now fixed. These were the new leaders who were expected to reform and rejuvenate Persia. The last of the Ghajar Kings had been sent to France for a "cure", and it was obvious now that he would never be asked to come back. These men were flatteringly called 'men of ideals' and among them was a man of destiny. Suddenly becoming glamourous and much sought after, they dined out every night and gambled at the card tables. To gain favour, some shady characters, of both sexes, jumped on the bandwagon and this aspect of the affair must have been a nightmare for the wives who, being respectable, were naturally barred from all parties except for the family ones. The wives simply had no way of knowing what their men were up to - and some of them must have longed for a quiet provincial appointment.

Although I was too young to understand, by chance I had an oblique glance at a very innocent example.

One day my father announced that he had been invited to a Christian New Year's party by the Russian community in Tehran. The odd thing about it was that my mother was also invited. Papa insisted that she should go with him. She declined, saying that she could not possibly go in a veil and all that. Father said, "Why not have a European costume made for the occasion and leave your *chador* behind in the car?" Mother did not give in but suggested that he could take me and my sister to this party instead.

We were warmly received and taken to a large room joined to another by a sliding door. Here, middle-aged blond ladies, neatly dressed and most of them wearing some jewellery were seated on chairs arranged against the walls. Dispersed among them were whiskered and high-collared gentlemen. They spoke in a guttural language to Papa and smiled at us. Some looked grave, but there was no hint of perpetual exile or misery among them. It had been only a short time since the Russian Revolution and, according to a Persian-speaking guest, "they were confident that the Bolshevik robbers would soon destroy themselves!". It was the first time I had heard the word "Bolshevik" and it didn't mean anything to me, but 'robbers' was most exciting and we kept asking Papa about them, but he didn't answer.

What delighted my sister and me was a number of young girls with lovely golden hair who were perpetually smiling and offering us food and drink. They had bare arms and golden arm-bands, the nearest thing to angels we had ever seen. They took us round a tree which twinkled like a star, and gave us two beautiful packets of bonbons. In the car on my way home I cried, saying I missed my mother. I must have been vaguely aware of the oppressive custom which barred my mother from such lovely parties and would bar me when I became a woman.

24

Chapter 10

EDUCATION

There was no doubt now that I was alive. Boredom is a very real and earthy feeling.

To be born a female in a Moslem state was just bad luck and no one could deny it. A woman was subject to every restriction, including the use of the *chador*, a thick black sack covering one from head to foot, when one appeared in public from the age of seven onwards. Men and women led separate lives, had their meals and amusements apart. In great households eunuchs acted as a link between the two sexes. In smaller ones there was a subtle system of *mahram* (the allowed ones) going between men and women. My father, brothers, uncles and male cousins were, for instance, *mahram* to me but not to my girl friend. Boys, before they reached puberty, were ideal *mahrams* and the presence of a white-haired woman was not considered improper in the men's apartment. How I longed sometimes to go out into the road and kick a ball with my brother's rowdy playmates, but that was out of the question.

My mother had a simple formula for bringing up girls. She would do to us as she had been done to. She would bring us up to be tough and patient and to know our place in society - a man's society, where there was no room for a silly or a weak woman. We would be taught the essence of Islam, good house management and perhaps also to read and write, although writing had not been encouraged in her days, as it might have led to surreptitious correspondence. And when, at the age of fourteen (her own age at her wedding), we would be married off as eligible young maidens, she hoped (without immodesty) we would bring as much credit to our parents as she had done to hers.

Far from becoming virtuous ladies, my sisters and I were growing into large louts and getting in everyone's way. So it was decided to insert us quietly into the classroom of my brothers' tutor. He was a charming middle-aged gentleman who wore an *aba* (loose gown) and a black turban in the manner of all clerics. He came twice a week to supply some grammar to the terrorists. Although my brothers talked of him as a tyrant, he was very gentle with my sister Zari and me. We sat on a bench and listened to the boys' incantation. Once he remarked that we looked like two little mice sitting on a large bar of soap. In due course, we were asked to copy out some squiggly lines on a piece of paper. It wasn't too bad.

There was another and a much more interesting tutor in the house. He was a grey-haired and white-faced creature who lived like a bat in the damp basement of the office villa. I now think he must have been a refugee from the Bolsheviks who had, like many other White Russians, found his way into Tehran and insinuated himself into the basement, claiming to teach the boys French and Russian in exchange for his keep and pocket money. My brothers insisted that he knew neither language, and judging by their own performance, or rather, lack of it, this must have been true. His name was Boukélyon and I learnt later that he had been a member of the French Academy. But we used to call him the monster and used to flatten our noses against his dusty basement windows just to see him angrily waving his arms and legs in the air. We were told that he always complained about food and used to call Persian cream cheese "salty froth of the sea" and stamp on it in rage.

One day during the Persian lessons an elaborate tea was served and we were told by the tutor that this would be his last lesson to us. Our father had arranged for him a good teaching post at a school in Rasht, where his family came from, and he was gratefully moving there. Naturally we were pleased that there would be no more lessons and the boys hurrahed after he left, but our pleasure did not last long.

My mother made enquiries and learnt from a cousin that her children were in the hands of a teaching mullah called Sheikh Baagher.

"Can he be trusted with young girls?" she asked.

"Very much so," was the reply. "He is a tyrant and gives them hell."

"Good! He is engaged."

The new teacher was not a tyrant. He was maniac. We recognised it the first time we saw him. Aged about twenty-five, he had green blazing eyes, a brutish face and thick hands. He wore an *aba* and a dirty white turban. I would not have allowed him within a mile of my children, but for some reason, he was considered suitable and began giving us regular lessons in writing and grammar. My two brothers who were now attending school dropped out, but my younger sister Maryam, aged five, had joined the class.

On the first day he began by producing a *ghalam-dan*, or decorated pencil box, from under his *aba*, opened it and took out some special dry reeds. Then he took out his pocketknife and began cutting them to a point. Some points were thick, some thin. He explained that the thick point was only used for *sarmashgh*, or sample writing, and the thin for normal writing. Then he asked us if we could find him an old cotton sock, which we did. He undid a few rows of the sock, soaked the long thread in water, and squeezing it into a tight ball, put it inside the empty inkpot. He told us that one must not use wool thread as it does not allow for a clean script. Then he opened a small bottle of Persian ink, called *morakab*, and poured it on the thread in the inkpot, saying it was a good, healthy mixture and one could even lick it off, unlike the European ink which was poisonous. Finally, when it was all ready, he took his pen, dipped it in the ink, and wrote a few elongated words in large letters in our exercise books saying that we were to copy them neatly fourteen times on every page. A servant brought in tea and biscuits. He drank the tea noisily, emptied the biscuits into his handkerchief, and left. We closed our books and scattered.

On Thursday afternoon my sisters and I were making rather a lot of noise. Suddenly Nanny said "What is all this noise? Why aren't you doing your homework? Your teacher is coming in about an hour."

Lord! We had forgotten all about it. We rushed and found our notebooks. The squiggly lines were stranger than ever. We could not make head or tail of them and asked if our mother could help. She was out. None of the servants could read. The inkpot had dried out and had to be moistened. Now the small reeds could not be found. Eventually we set to work but were defeated by the elaborate lines. The next best thing was to copy each word in a row downwards. The rows got crooked. Remembering our teacher's words about the wholesomeness of the ink, we licked it off and wrote again. This time the ink spread. We forgot the dots or put in too many. By the time we reached the end of the page it was a filthy mess.

There was no time to finish it all. The mullah was there and demanding to see our work. He took one look at the notebooks and his face paled, his green eyes became bloodshot. He reached for one hefty shoe, which he had taken off on entering the room, and hit me on the shoulder with it. He broke a ruler over my younger sister's head, and slapped my elder sister with both his hands.

There was bedlam. We were screaming and he was hitting out in all directions. I had never seen anyone so angry. Then he took our notebooks, tore the pages out, and scattered them all over the floor. I can't remember any more of that nightmare lesson except that at the end of it we had to pick up all the bits of paper which he had thrown over the carpet.

It was impossible to please the man as we could not understand the point of copywriting, the chanting and the Arabic grammar. After the first blows, we were usually too confused and numb with fear to take in anything. He had the sadistic habit of putting a pencil between our knuckles and pressing our fingers together. I could scarcely bear the pain myself, but when it was inflicted on my younger sister, I got frantic and ran about the room calling for help.

So Thursdays and Mondays became a regular hell. We begged Nanny to intervene and ask my mother to stop the lessons. She said that she was not allowed to interfere, but if we yelled loud enough my mother might hear us and dismiss the man. To our disappointment we found that the louder we screamed, the harder we were beaten. There was nothing for it but patience.

Chapter 11

PHANTOM DINNER PARTIES

Thursday, however, had its compensation. Being Friday Eve, which is particularly significant to practising Moslems, the family ghosts usually left their resting places and came for a brief visit. They hovered overhead or sat on the garden wall, listening to every conversation and watching the family's activities. They approved of pious acts such as the cooking of huge quantities of food to be given to the poor.

These ancestors rarely manifested their presence, but nevertheless, everyone knew that they were there. They were mostly ancient Cossacks with long beards and voracious appetites. They each had their preference, and the menu was arranged according to their likes and dislikes when they had been alive.

Our preference, however, was for a ghost with a sweet tooth, who could only be satisfied with *halva* or *sholézard* - the one made from flour, sugar and saffron; the other from rice, sugar and saffron. These confections were made in huge tinned copper vessels called *deegs* and cooked on a low flame for hours, giving out a most delicious perfume supposed to attract ghosts, even stray ones sometimes.

Sholézard, a bright yellow pudding, was poured into small blue earthenware bowls and the surface of the pudding decorated with thin lines of ground cinnamon in the shape of pious words, such as Allah. As the Hamadan bowls were extremely cheap they were often given away with the contents.

Halva, on the other hand, had to be rocked like a baby in a cradle until oil oozed out of every pore, then it was made into small balls while still hot and flattened on a plate. Then either religious verses were inscribed on it with the point of a knife, or a pretty pattern made with the edge of a spoon. Thus prepared, the dishes were taken out into the streets by veiled women who held them out to the passers-by. Anyone wishing to take a fingerful had to say a *salavat*, or blessing, on the spirit the dish was dedicated to. Naturally, the dispenser sought out the poorest as they were more numerous and the return in blessing, more voluminous. They avoided the smart people and never let the infidels touch the stuff as their touch would make it impure for the rest.

In this connection, my aunt had a very odd experience. She once dreamt of her dead father and asked him how he was. He replied "Hungry". She immediately set to work and made his favourite *aush*, a thick soup with rice, meat and vegetables. This was served to a group of mendicants at the door. Amongst these was a poor Armenian who received a bowl of *aush*, but no spoon, as the touch of his tongue would have made it unclean. A few nights later my aunt dreamt of her father and asked him, "How did you like your *aush*?" He replied, "Well enough, but the bowl burnt my mouth."

Chapter 12

THE TIGER STOPS

My father's fall from power, when it came, was not spectacular in the context of Persian politics, as great heights were not involved. But it was interesting in two respects. First, it signalled the disruption of the band of brothers and the emergence of one-man rule. Secondly, it was the beginning of a skimming purge which left a famine of independent political figures in the country for two decades.

Father was a political innocent who believed that collective government was possible without any individual being subservient to any other. He also recognised that our country needed extensive reforms and modernisation, which only the genius of Reza Khan was capable of bringing about. The two men were staunch friends and that friendship was a source of hope and inspiration to him. Reza Khan, clear-headed, brave and impatient; Papa humane, slow and patient somehow complemented one another.

One day at a Cabinet meeting, a letter marked "Urgent" was handed to Reza Khan. He read it, glowered at my father, and left the room.

That night, Papa was arrested and taken to Ghasre Ghajar, a notorious dungeon. For three months he was interrogated about his relations with the exiled Ahmad Shah. He just could not understand what his tormentors wanted. Eventually he was shown a letter alleged to have been confiscated on its way out of Persia. This letter purported to be from a secret group of loyalists in Tehran to the exiled King in France, assuring him of their support if he wished to return and reassert himself, and indicating that my father might be prepared to pave the way for his return. The letter had no signature, the supporting group remained anonymous, and the only name mentioned was that of my father. The date and the place of the letter's interception were not disclosed, and the only clue to its discovery was the name of a Foreign Office official who, as it happened, was my father's only enemy.

Meanwhile, my family was in a state of panic. There was no telling what would happen in that dreadful gaol. My mother had a great deal of support from relations and some friends, but the majority of the new friends melted away.

One evening my mother was told that she had a lady visitor who refused to give her name. When the person was taken into the reception room and left alone with my mother, the thick *chador* was discarded and out came the black beard of an old acquaintance of Papa's. He was a thin, cautious man, a natural courtier who had a foot in each camp. My mother laughed and said, "What makes you wear a *chador*, Sir?" The friend was very agitated and kept looking behind him. He said, "Your house is surrounded by spies and informers. I could not possibly let them recognise me. I have just come to assure you that we are all active on behalf of the General, but you must also help. Go and see Reza Khan yourself, or send your children, as often as you can. Demand an open trial for your husband. We are certain that he would be cleared if there was a trial.

My mother was not quite sure whether she could trust him, but decided there was no harm in putting on the pressure.

After three months, father was allowed to come home, but only as a prisoner under house arrest in his office villa. The officer in charge of the guards (all of whom, incidentally, we had to feed) was charming, and allowed an occasional visit by my mother and brothers. Suddenly Papa was released. There had been no trial and there was no stain, only a great permanent wound.

Chapter 13

THE PROPERTY

After the hue and cry was over, my father decided to settle down to a quiet life in the country and try his hand at farming. This idea was encouraged by his wealthy friend, Amir-Monazam, who himself had begun farming successfully in what would be the equivalent of a home county within daily reach of the capital. He mentioned that his neighbouring village was for sale and was worth looking at.

A freehold village in Persia is not a parish; nor is it a green and delightful rural community with roads, private houses, retired admirals, and the rule of law. It is a vast or large expanse of land divided into fields, vineyards and orchards. The villagers, in those days, were sold with the land, but were not serfs and could leave the village if they wished to, but could not sell the land that they cultivated as it was not theirs.

They usually lived in what was called a *ghaleh* or fortress. This was an area surrounded by a high wall and entered by a gate on top of which was a flimsy, mud-built lookout and fortifications. The village street, some six yards wide and a few hundred yards long, would run the length of the *ghaleh* and would be flanked by the doorways of mud houses. Each house had two rooms, a yard with a shallow pool, and a cattle shed. Most villages had their own water-mill which generally served as a meeting place and some lucky villages had their *Imam-Zadeh*, or consecrated mosque, where a forgotten saint had been buried.

My father and his friends went in two cars to see the property. The twenty miles or so to Karaj on the so-called *chaussée* road was pretty poor going and they had to stop to deal with two punctures. But after Karaj, where they met Amir-Monazam and a guide, the road ceased altogether. The guide had to go ahead on foot and search for the least pot-holey part of the track. The cars travelling at a snail's pace, were boiling constantly and water had to be poured into the radiators from large cans. Yadollah and Abbas, the two drivers, not unnaturally assumed disproportionate importance on this trip.

As the party approached the village perimeter they saw a dark shadow near a group of barren service trees. This was the group of villagers - all sixteen of them - burying the last of the village children in the village graveyard, a flattened field dotted by mud-brick headstones. The wind was blowing and minute dust storms were raised into the air. A desolate youth was beating monotonously on a drum at long intervals. The village mullah was leading a prayer around the open grave. No one took any notice of the bareheaded woman who was rubbing her hair in the dust and wailing for her lost boy.

As the emaciated dogs barked, the villagers turned sharply round in the direction of the noise and seeing the two monstrous vehicles moving towards them ran away in panic - all but the *kad-khoda*, the village head, who had been to Karaj several times and seen such a monster. It was called *hotol-mobin* (automobile) and drank oil. He recognised the guide and was told the purpose of the visit. He welcomed the visitors and explained that he would attend to them as soon as the business in hand was over.

"What business is that?" he was asked.

"We are burying the last of the village infants. God gives them and takes them away. They never stay with us for long."

He took the party to the open grave. They looked in and saw a little red bundle lying at the bottom.

"Did he die of an accident?"

"No. He was snatched by As-Ma-Behtaran (better than us) ghosts who haunt lonely places."

"But why is he all red."

"Oh, that; we had no shroud left in the village so the mother wrapped the child in her own scarf."

"Tell me, how do you recognise the grave of your relatives as there is no name on any of the headstones?"

"So long as our eyes are wet, the new grave is recognised by its dampness. By the time the earth dries, so does our grief. Besides, there is no point in writing as none of us can read, not even the village mullah."

The villagers had gradually and timidly reappeared and were eyeing the newcomers curiously, but kept at a respectful distance from the cars.

Someone was shovelling earth into the grave. The *kad-khoda* mentioned the men's names and pointed to their spheres of cultivation in the distance. There were no surnames and all the men were known only by one or two Mohammedan names.

"This boy, Karim, the drummer, is now the youngest in the village. He is ten and a shepherd; Roghieh is expecting a child any day now," pointing to a bundle of rags, "so there will be children again."

When the burial was over, the headman took the party on an extensive tour of the village. Every building had either fallen down or was badly in need of repair. The central point of the village, the water-mill, had stopped functioning a few months before for lack of water and this, the men explained, was due to the ancient *ghanat* silting up.

A *ghanat* is a deep subterranean reservoir in the highlands from which water is eventually brought to the surface by means of an underground tunnel. This involves digging a number of wells each less deep than the previous one at intervals in a direct line from the reservoir until the water surfaces in a spring, usually in a ravine.

The *ghanat* supplying this village had long ago fallen into decay. Tiles had fallen in, blocking the watercourse. The ravine had become marshy and overgrown with reeds, alive with frogs and water snakes. A few water buffaloes waded in the slime and a million mosquitoes buzzed overhead.

34

"Phew!" cried Aziz-Olah Khan, the army doctor who had accompanied the party, "I wouldn't touch this place with a barge pole unless you want your whole family to die of malaria. If this is their drinking water, no wonder the children don't stay here long."

But the *moghani* (well-sinker) and the land agent were not so pessimistic about the place. They seemed to think that the hills to the east of the village were "damp", or potentially water-producing, and did not rule out the possibility of making another *ghanat*. But on the whole, everyone agreed that it was a poor property. On the way back, one of the cars broke its back axle, and the other got stuck while fording the river Mard-Abad. The party had to walk a few miles and spend the night at Ghale Nou, a lively and prosperous village belonging to Amir-Monazam. Here, I think, my father talked it over with his friend who persuaded him to buy the place. It was going very cheaply and had a few thousand acres of cultivable land; if only a new water supply could be provided, one could transform the ruins. I like to believe that Papa was moved by the fate of the wretched inhabitants and felt he could to some degree help them. He certainly was attracted by the challenge.

I was watching my mother squeeze medicinal oil from ground almonds when I first heard the name Meshkin-Abad mentioned.

"What a peculiar name! Why is it called Meshkin-Abad, I wonder?" she asked.

"We don't know," said the Major. "One can only imagine that the name derived from *bid-meshk* (a pussy willow, which was the source of a perfumed distillation), one of the few types of trees which grow freely in that village."

"Who is the present owner?"

"A very dissolute aristocrat entitled 'Obedient to the King'. He comes from an ancient line. His father owned seventy-three villages at the time of his death. The son has blown them all through his opium pipe. There are two more to go."

As the Major rattled on about the property, I had a child's vivid picture of a miniature village attaining gas form and being squeezed through a hole in a porcelain pipe to come out in a bubble. As it grew, numerous sheep and shepherds stepped out of the balloon and on contact with the air burst like soap bubbles at a touch. How could a man smoke a village? It seemed very odd indeed.

They were still talking when my vision dimmed and my hearing was restored.

The Major had apparently given an *eskenas* (paper money) to the bereaved woman who had looked at it uninterestedly and had asked him what it was. He had said, "This is money. Buy yourself something with it." She had looked at him angrily, and replied, "We villagers are simple but not fools. Money is a coin of gold or silver. It is this shape," bringing the tip of her thumb and forefinger together.

He laughed without comprehension.

Chapter 14

GHALE NOU

Between the start of the First World War and the middle of the 1920s a new wave of émigrés reached Tehran. These were refugees from the chaos in Russia, many of them Moslems from the Southern provinces. They were not exactly destitute and were extremely well educated. They were, therefore, immediately absorbed into the primitive economy where men with practical knowledge of industry and commerce were rare and badly needed. They started banks, civil engineering firms, commercial and industrial organisations. While their Moslem ancestry made them socially acceptable and their university education gave them an advantage, their European outlook enlivened a rigidly Moslem society. This group was collectively called "The Caucasians".

My parents had many friends amongst them, and they were fortunate in having the most celebrated of the Caucasians as their best friend. He was what I always like to think of as the last aristocrat, a type driven out of Europe by the vulgarities of the Twentieth Century. His ancestors were distinguished Seyeds from Baku. He left Russia in his late twenties and settled in Tehran. Within ten years he had made a fortune, received a title and married into a great family. But if you are about to raise an eyebrow, don't, because he was not a slick operator. Tall and handsome, with great intelligence and love of beauty, he built the two most beautiful houses in the Avenue Shah with magnificent staircases and galleries. He laid out the gardens with ornamental statues which it was unusual to find in Tehran in those days. Later, one of these houses was used as the premises of the Scandinavian Club.

He had a hand in modernising the Persian Fisheries, although he hated fish and never allowed it to enter his house. So while he collected handsome remuneration from the fisheries, Mama received all the delicious caviar and salmon which were, from time to time, sent to him but diverted to our kitchen before he could smell them.

He was the only man I knew who could, with dignity, introduce his latest child to you without mentioning the child's mother. If one were churlish enough to ask who the child's mother was, he would reply icily, "Madame, naturally". No one as far as I knew ever had the nerve to ask "Which?"

While my father was serving as Minister of the Interior, they had met and become friends and they loved one another to the end of their lives.

So now he asked us to stay in his country house in Ghale Nou for as long as it was necessary while we built our house in Meshkin-Abad.

His house was a handsome, two-storey brick and wood building with panelled ceilings and walls, all painted white. There were balconies overlooking flower gardens, unfamiliar washbasins and European-style lavatories which took one by surprise. It was altogether like being in paradise. My parents left Maryam, my youngest sister, in Tehran and took Zari and me with them, as well as my brothers Ismail and Jamshid.

During the evening the grown-ups discussed what was most essential to get Meshkin-Abad habitable as quickly as possible. They agreed that the first priority was to make the track from Karaj to Meshkin-Abad into a passable road and to repair a small shelter for the family to stay in while the house was being built.

The next morning we were awakened by loud singing. Looking out of the window, we saw in the backyard four large women, two on each side of a wooden tripod, from which was suspended what looked like a huge goat slung on its back. They were pushing the creature to and fro and singing with all their might. My mother explained that this was not a real goat but the skin of one filled with fresh unskimmed yoghurt to which water was added and then it was rocked until butter was formed. The neck was then gently opened and a hand put in to draw out the butter in large pats. The remaining skimmed yoghurt was then either drunk as *doogh* or boiled until it became a hard substance called *kashk*, whereupon it was dried in the sun and used in the winter for cooking.

Someone was baking bread, someone else was piling white mulberries on trays for breakfast; it all looked so jolly and lively. After breakfast we were shown the orchards, the cow sheds, the chicken houses with enormous eggs. Everything was spick and span and well looked after.

Later on, mules were provided to take us for our first view of the new property, but my sister and I shared a donkey. We took the short cut which was approximately three miles. On the way, Papa said to my mother, "You must not expect anything as flourishing as Ghale Nou, but I hope we will eventually make something of the place." It must have been the greatest understatement of his life!

So as not to depress my mother on her first visit, Papa asked the muleteer to avoid passing the cemetery, so we made a detour and rode through a narrow footpath in an orchard till we came in front of the water-mill. Straight in front, down the drive was our country seat. The drive itself was quite pretty with pussy willows alternating with different species of roses - a poet's work no doubt. At the end of the drive, however, there was nothing but a high wall which had fallen down in several places, terminating at each end in a ruined watchtower.

"Well," said my mother, "this is not very jolly, but let us go in and see if the house can be patched up."

"But there is no house. I told you, if you remember, and there is not much of a garden either."

"So what is to be done? No house, no garden, not even drinking water. Where do we go from here?" She looked very downcast.

"We must decide where to start tackling it. Where, for instance, shall we build a house?" he answered mildly.

After hours of investigation, they decided first to repair the walls of the garden, so as to enclose an area of about half a square-mile and to repair the north-eastern tower for temporary residence.

We spread our rugs and ate our bread, cheese and boiled eggs and Mama was just about to have a siesta when a group of women stepped in through the gap in the wall. They greeted my mother and put before her a few eggs in a basket and a handkerchief full of *naané-ghandi*, or sweetened bread apologizing that it was the only gift they could offer. Mama was so touched that she burst into tears. She had completely forgotten the villagers and had come empty-handed. She promised to bring them lengths of cloth, tea and sugar next time she visited the village. This formality over, we thought the women would leave, but they hung about and Mama although tired, sat out of politeness, talking to them. We were now being pestered by flies so we got up to have another look round, but were followed everywhere by the women. Mama, rather exasperated, whispered, "I hope we're not always going to be followed about like this", to which my father answered, "This is because they have not seen a new face for a long time. I expect they will eventually tire of ours."

Chapter 15

BORJ

The *borj* (tower), when repaired, was delightful. It was round and had four windows pointing towards the four directions of the compass. No glass was used in the building and there were shutters to regulate the amount of sun and light needed at any time. For the first time I began to notice the shadows of the countryside and the distant mountains. The colours of the morning, noon and evening were all different.

We stayed for a few weeks at Ghale Nou and joined my parents in the daily trek to and from the village. It was not so bad riding the donkey, but sometimes we had to walk and although the morning walk was easy enough, the miles seemed to double on the return trip, and we could hardly drag our feet. Papa often carried one or the other of us on his back for a short distance.

The *borj*, although tall, was only one room on top of a storage room, and was all we had for eating and sleeping in. It was reached by a flight of wooden stairs from the garden. There was a small landing on which my mother cooked our meals on a primus stove in the evenings. During the day we spent all our time out of doors. In the storeroom we kept paraffin for hurricane lamps, guns, gardening implements, and a barrelful of fermenting, sour-smelling stuff. We washed in the little brook which entered from under the garden wall and ran the length of the garden. Every day a donkey brought our drinking water in four large earthenware jars from Ghale Nou.

Every morning, as soon as we woke up, our bedding was whisked away, folded and wrapped in red and white check homespun sheets, which were then placed against the chalk walls as cushions. By this time Ismail and Jamshid who were in charge of "fire" had reddened some charcoal for the samovar. This was done by lighting a rag and putting it among the charcoal placed in a small wire basket with a lid, called *atesh charkhan*. This was attached to a long wire and spun quickly in the air. As it gathered momentum it looked at times like a small satellite whizzing round the child's head. The boys loved doing this. My mother then spread a cloth on the carpet and when the water in the samovar began to boil, she opened the tap and poured the boiling water on the tea leaves. She then placed the pot on top of the samovar to brew slightly. With tea we had bread and cream cheese and sometimes boiled milk.

After breakfast, a village woman would come in to wash the dishes in the running stream, sweep the carpet in the *borj* and cook something for lunch on an improvised, out-of-doors stove, while my parents supervised the clearing of the garden and the planning of the new house. As the rubbish was cleared, bit by bit the outline of the original garden began to appear.

40

Here, I must explain that a country house garden in Persia is nothing like an English garden with lawns, lakes and a landscaped park. It is purely functional, containing orchards, vineyards, herb and vegetable gardens and an open air melon culture called *safy-kari*. The produce is primarily for sale and for the use of the family. This had originally been a rectangular enclosure half a mile wide by one and a half long. On each corner there had been a *borj* exactly like the one we now occupied. According to the *kad-khoda*, there had also been a gate and fortifications on the north wall and, presumably, living quarters which had long since disappeared. Two-thirds of the distance along the long wall there was a wide arch under which the river Ostour ran the width of the garden and came out on the other side. On the further side of the river was a complete wilderness and, although it was within the walled enclosure, I don't think I ever explored it.

In the summer, the river was reduced to a trickle by the time it reached us, but the banks had to be wide enough to allow for spring flooding. Many wild creatures got through under the arch in the dry season and there were traces of jackals, foxes, hyenas, and even wolves in winter. Thus, there was a need for another protective wall. We were told, in any case, not to wander beyond the permitted area and especially not to go near the ruins as these were "crawling with snakes and scorpions". This, I am afraid, completely put us off.

Lunch was generally meagre. As there was no meat in the village, we had to make do with gruel, bread and yoghurt. Papa sometimes shot a duck, or a few pigeons, and our eastern neighbour, the owner of Farokh-Abad, sent us a deer which was delicious when roasted on charcoal.

By the time the evening came we were too exhausted to want anything much. The boys lit the hurricane lamps and Mama fried eggs on the primus stove on the landing. We often heard howling noises from beyond the walls but were told that it was only the wind. Papa opened an old flask and had a sip of some strong-smelling water whilst the boys played cards by the light of the hurricane lamps. We fell asleep.

The days were getting warmer, and it was necessary to have a rest after midday. Once, when my parents were having a siesta, we were told to go into the garden if we could not keep quiet. I found myself in the storeroom with my two brothers, dreamily handling cartridges and things. The barrel's contents stank. I asked Ismail if we could clean it out.

He said, "No. Father wants to drink it."

"What? This foul stuff? It will poison him."

"Of course he won't drink it as it is, you silly. He would first cook it in some glass tube that would make it clean."

"I still think it would taste horrid. Can you shoot?"

"Of course I can shoot. I helped Papa shoot those pigeons."

"Will you shoot me then?"

My younger brother, Jamshid, and I stood in the doorway, side by side, grinning idiotically as though we were being photographed. Ismail picked up a gun and aimed it at us. He put his finger on the trigger, then, suddenly, as though he had second thoughts, he turned his back to us and pulled the trigger. There was a loud explosion and we saw daylight through a vast hole in the wall.

A few days later we all went to Tehran as we were in need of a bath.

Chapter 16

ROSES

My father's idea of a country house was very simple. So long as the rooms were large and the ceilings high, he was quite satisfied, provided there were enough cupboards and the rooms were uncluttered with knick-knacks. In response to a suggestion that the house-plan should be drawn up by an architect, I heard him protest "What for? I don't want a palace, just a few rooms to shelter from the midday sun. Anyway, we shall be out of doors most of the time. And besides, the cost must be kept down as a lot needs rebuilding in the village."

So the local builder had his way. He built a small L-shaped house on a raised platform. It was one-storeyed, but looked like two from outside as it was so high. Two broad verandas ran the length of the house on the east and the west on to which the French windows opened. The ceilings consisted of pale, rough beams of poplar wood laid under a layer of woven straw matting. The walls were covered in plaster and whitewashed. We had flagstones on the floors and the doors were made from pale poplar wood and left unpainted. There was a flat roof of mud reinforced with straw, which we jokingly called the guests' dormitory.

At the far end of the garden, against the south wall, were built a series of drab-looking rooms, which were to house the dairy, the *tanur* or bakery, the indoor kitchen, and the servants' quarters. Another group of buildings were put up outside the garden on the left of the drive. This group contained a large garage and chauffeur's quarters, barns, a dove house, a brick kiln and stables.

It is extraordinary that I cannot remember the house being built. It was as though one day everything sprang up by magic. Reed curtains, horizontally woven, hung outside the open windows. Rough wooden tables and divans, made by a local carpenter, and canvas chairs furnished the rooms. Some familiar Persian carpets had found their way on to the floors, Azra and Nanny were there, and the whole affair was wondrous.

My first recollection of the house will always be connected with roses - baskets and baskets full of rose-heads picked first thing in the morning and brought to my mother to distil rose water from. I often wonder whether the roses were a symbol of a happy period in my parents' life when every day was marked by some interesting or useful activity? Certainly, my parents had found the right outlet for their middle-aged energies. A programme was now arranged and days were set aside for routine work, and those to spare were filled with seasonal and unexpected events.

On Mondays, bread was baked in the *tanur*, a single cylindrically-shaped tile sunk into the earth. It was some three feet deep and eighteen inches in diameter. At dawn, a great deal of wood was burnt inside it and the flames gradually allowed to die down. The *tanur* was tested several times until it was found to have reached the right temperature. Then a woman flattened balls of leavened dough and handed them to the baker - another woman (usually pregnant) would sit at the edge of the inferno and stretch the flattened dough very quickly on a curved wooden shield covered with muslin and, bending down, stick the dough on to the hot tile of the *tanur*. By the time she stuck a second disc, the first was ready to come out. She would bend right down again and with one movement strip it with a long pair of tongs and produce a large oval-shaped wafer of thin bread, smelling heavenly. This was *naané lavash* and was left out to cool before it was stacked and put away. On occasions like this all the women in the household helped and, naturally, my sisters and I also wanted to watch the proceedings, which worried my mother terribly. It was assumed that children could fall in the *tanur*, which meant certain death, whereas adults couldn't. Eventually, a place was allocated to us near the door and we were threatened with expulsion if we took another step inside. Sometimes milk-bread and fancy biscuits were made for breakfast, then we were given a board and allowed to flatten out small balls of pastry. That was fun.

Butter-making day was also amusing. There was no pasteurisation yet in Persia; the cheapest and simplest method of preserving milk was to turn it into yoghurt and then butter. This was churned in the regulation slung goat skin, and we would have loved to have spent our energies shaking the creature, but Medina, who was in charge of the operation, was obviously prejudiced. She believed that my footsteps were heavy and if I walked within sight of the tripod, butter would refuse to form inside the silly goat, whereas my sister had light footsteps and was allowed to walk up and down. I did not care for this attitude.

Distillation of roses and pussy willow was divine to begin with but boring on account of its slowness. The petals were picked first thing in the morning and filled the rooms by the time we woke up. By nine o'clock they were pressed inside a huge *deeg* which had a special lid with pipes attached to it and was made to simmer slowly on an outdoor open-fronted clay oven. After a long time a liquid began dribbling out of the pipe. This was collected in a basin, and then was poured into demijohns, which were corked with cotton wool and sealed with plaster later. My sisters and I daubed as much of these sweet waters as we could on our persons, making ourselves smell like sorbets and Persian puddings.

Meanwhile, Papa bought himself several fat account books and entered his expenses there. Naturally, there were no profits yet. He also bought a herd of donkeys in order to start a courier service to the capital. These were large undoctored brutes, who made a dreadful noise and kicked and bit. The flock of sheep increased and Karim, playing his reed pipe, led them like the Pied Piper.

My father usually left the house after breakfast taking along Jamshid and Ismail and went to inspect the work of the clearing up, the seed sowing and the building of the new *ghanat*. Everything now depended upon water being found in quantity, and everyone was praying for it. Meanwhile he built a community centre for the village. Opposite the Ghale (where the villagers lived) and across from the brook which passed its doors, a small dusty *maidan* was flattened out. On one side of it, a mosque and a school were built, and on the other side a public bath.

The combined mosque-school was very odd. It was rather like an outsized municipal bus shelter, built on a platform and having two sides, back to back, so to speak. On one side, men would kneel in prayer and on the other, children would chant their alphabets.

The unconsecrated mosque was never much patronised, although Papa appointed a muezzin to call people to prayer. He called faithfully at sunrise and sunset, but his midday calls were erratic. Having no clock in the village, he just climbed the mud roof when he got home to lunch. One day mother noticed that he called as late as two o'clock, therefore invalidating everyone's midday devotions. To this Papa replied that the poor man had been harvesting and God would no doubt stretch a point on that occasion.

The school did not fare any better. The mullah, the only available "intellectual", was a poor, white-bearded dimwit, who could hardly read or write. He only knew how to grow poplars and that did not help. It was suggested that he should take lessons from my father and prepare himself to become the future schoolmaster. Invariably, he arrived at our house at seven o'clock in the evening with long, incoherent stories of the past which no one could make head or tail of. He found it impossible to distinguish between similar consonants and kept on interrupting the lessons by repeating a chapter of the Koran he had learnt by heart. Eventually, father got so bored that he gave the man written permission to teach whatever village children there were to be found.

The public bath, architecturally speaking, was much less primitive. It had a dressing room, two sunken reservoirs for hot and cold water (later on, someone swore that he had seen frogs and water snakes in the cold reservoir), and a boiler heated by a wood fire. Finally - a professional finish - the glass skylights of the three domes peeped out of the mud roof.

Everyone was delighted with this new luxury. It was going to be heated one day a week for men, one day for women and one day for the master's family. But at the moment there was no water, so it had to wait.

The water, when it came, nearly caused a tragedy. A deep well was dug and when the supply was found to be adequate, they began digging shafts, and eventually a tunnel was made from the end of the gorge where the water was due to surface to within feet of the main source. Over a thousand lengths of clay pipes, like macaroni sections, were laid end to end in the tunnel. All that was needed was to dig through the last few feet and reach the spring. When this happened, the force of water was such that it swept the poor tunneller off his feet and nearly carried him away. He was saved by his mate who had more experience of *ghanat* digging. Immediately, men were sent to the village where two fat sheep had been tethered for a week ready to be sacrificed. They were taken to the watercourse, where they were slaughtered. Their blood, washed away by the pure water of the *ghanat*, was meant to prevent human life from being lost.

Everyone came and dipped their hands in the icy, clear water of the *ghanat*. Some wept, not knowing why.

That night the village celebrated. They roasted one of the carcasses and ate it round a bonfire. Then they smoked their long clay pipes filled with cheap tobacco. Like all good Moslems they had no alcoholic drinks. Two young men sang with clear and beautiful voices. We could hear them from our garden.

46

The restrained happiness of the villagers had moved my parents. Papa was overcome with excitement. He kept pacing the veranda saying that he had not known such complete satisfaction before, that it was far better than winning a campaign as it left no losers.

The village had received a new lease of life. The tunneller had estimated the volume of water as several *sangs*. Each *sang*, or stone, is a measure of water needed to turn a large millstone. There was far more than we needed to irrigate our land.

The news of the *ghanat's* success soon spread. Next day we had a visit from Amir-Monazam and his family, and the following day the master of Farokh-Abad came to congratulate Papa. An atmosphere of optimism began to prevail.

One day towards evening, we were taken to the *borj* to watch the burning out of the old waterway. Gallons of paraffin were splashed on to the reeds which were then set alight. Great tongues of flame leapt up in the sky and, blown by the wind, crackled on until they covered the whole ridge of a hill, eventually settling down to an angry glow which blended with the setting sun on the north-western horizon.

I asked Jamshid what had happened to the water buffaloes. He replied: "Horrible brutes! I am afraid they were all saved."

Chapter 17

THE SERVANTS

Each time we visited Tehran everything seemed different. Somehow, our long stay in the country sharpened our appreciation of the city. The faces were a welcome change; the bustle was agreeable; even the cry of the street vendors was good to hear. After the first few minutes, the faces became familiar again and stayed so until our next homecoming.

There was grandmother, voluble as ever. Fatemeh Baji, the faithful housekeeper, irritable with the children as usual, rattled on in Turkish, giving Mama all the news; the Major, beaming with confidence, told Papa about his work at the Army treasury, about our friends' doings, and any changes in the Cabinet.

Soon after we arrived word got round, and friends and relatives called singly or in groups. Mama hardly seemed to leave her reception room for the first few days, and my father who received his guests in the *bironi*, or office villa, was in the same position. Tea and sherbets were perpetually made and served to the guests, and meals put back it seemed for hours. Jamshid believed that if you managed to put salt in the guests' shoes they would leave early, but it was as easy as putting salt on a bird's tail. We sometimes went to the drawing-room, behaved badly and were ordered out.

Most of the time that Mama was receiving visitors, we had to put up with the servants' company. The head of these was Fatemeh Baji, a "treasure" my parents had picked up in Ghazvin, where they were stationed some twenty years before. She had looked after their newborn son, Vali, and had shown such devotion that she was snatched up and brought to Tehran. Now she was a weird-looking septuagenarian, who ruled the servants and the children with an iron fist. First to be up and last to bed, she never spared herself or anyone else. As far as I remember, she was an ill-tempered old woman, perpetually stirring a stew and cooking rice in a smoke-filled kitchen. Whenever we made an uninvited visit, she would chase us out with a long pair of tongs. To Mama, she meant safety, security, law and order. We could leave the house for months knowing it was in good hands.

Next in order of importance came my Nanny. Most Persian nannies in my time were also wet nurses. The Persian name for it is *nané* or *dayé*. Dried or pasteurised milk was not yet known and the only way to keep alive a baby who could not be fed by its mother was to engage a wet nurse. Most large families who could afford it had wet nurses and those who couldn't had a high mortality rate.

This class of dependants was very cossetted. They received good food, long rest periods and no correction or unpleasantness, as that was supposed to dry up their supplies. Naturally, some of them behaved like *prima donnas*, but not my Nanny. Her life history was, to say the least, quite remarkable. She came from a professional family in Hamadan. Her father was a doctor. Unfortunately he was dead by the time she fell victim to smallpox at the age of eight. Her mother, who had been married three times and produced only one daughter, made a bargain with God. If she were to survive and not become blind she would be given in marriage to the first poor Seyed (descendant of Prophet Mohammed) who came along. She was lucky. Not only was she not blind, but her face and body were in no way marked by the disease and she grew into a most beautiful, tall girl. Her mother kept her bargain. At the age of eleven, Khadijeh was given in marriage to a poor and ne'er-do-well farming Seyed. She bore him several children of whom three boys survived and, with the help of her family, she kept him solvent. When her youngest child was a month old, she learnt that her husband had taken another wife during her pregnancy and was expecting another family soon. This so incensed her that she took her three boys and set out for the capital with very little money. She couldn't read or write and had never travelled alone before.

The hardship she suffered on that journey still brings a lump to my throat. In Hamadan she had met the wife and family of my uncle, the *Mirpange*, while he was stationed there. She liked them and knew that if she could find them in Tehran they would help. It is a measure of the size and intimacy of Tehran society at that time that without having their address she was able to find them.

When my aunt's eyes fell upon Khadijeh, with a babe in her arms, she exclaimed, "Providence has guided your steps here in order to save the life of the twins."

"Which twins?" inquired Khadijeh.

"My sister-in-law had twins a week ago and she cannot manage them both."

"Well, I can."

Apart from what, in the old days, was called her 'honour', she could never refuse anything. Even her life meant nothing to her. And so it was that my family acquired another treasure. She looked after the twins and fed Gohar as well as her own boy and when she was asked whether she would agree to a certain salary she replied, "I didn't know that human milk could be sold".

When Gohar was a year old, I was born. She was quickly put on solid food and I was given to Nanny. She gave me too much love.

She had long, slim hands that she used to dip into a bowl of water and, passing a hand lightly over a child's face like an act of blessing, with one downward stroke she cleaned and purified. She had a round face, lovely complexion and gentle brown eyes. She was grave with an air of distinction and although she did not laugh aloud, she was cheerful and never spoke crossly to anyone. Religious by nature and upbringing, she never missed a prayer, yet she was not censorious.

Maryam's young nanny, Dayé, was made in an entirely different mould. She was the life and soul of the house. Her laughter, like fireworks, exploded into showers of pleasure. She came from the mountain village of Demavand, where apples and girls share the same pink and white colour scheme. She, too, had been the victim of smallpox. Alas, she carried the marks on her face. She also had a limp. But her good nature and high spirits were such that these blemishes were hardly noticed. Married to a 'Gendarme' at an early age, she had had a girl who had died, and the 'Gendarme', wishing to improve his position, offered his wife as a wet nurse when he heard of the last addition to our family. Dayé, a mimic, storyteller, singer and dancer, would have made a name for herself as a professional entertainer had she been born in Europe. As it was, her talents only brightened our household.

I remember long evenings when something was going on and we were required to keep quiet. We were put in Dayé's charge, who would tell lengthy stories of magicians, kings and thieves, interspersed with relevant poems. It now puzzles me how an illiterate young village girl could know forms of speech used at court such as (addressing a king):

"May the 'Mecca of the Universe' remain in perpetual safety, the lives of these ruffians is not worth one hair of your Majesty's head." Or: "May your slave," meaning himself "be sacrificed to your slightest whim." People spoke of their son as "The light of my eyes", and of their wife as "The flower of my garden".

50

She had several rhyming animal stories. In most of them the animals and birds automatically knew all the secrets, that is why they were denied speech. This influenced me deeply. She also had a story about a poor girl who found a golden comb in a public bath. As a result she became a great personage until she lost the comb. The golden comb also stuck in my mind as a symbol, the opposite of the skeleton in the cupboard. If an old lady shows me a magnificent rose in her back graden, or a piece of porcelain, if a stranger talks about his son at Cambridge, or his fine collection of stamps, I remember the golden comb.

One particular floor show was our favourite especially on account of its improper ending. The lame nanny would tie her *chador* round her waist in the style of village women and do a song and dance, going through the whole natural cycle of cultivation from the time the seed was sown to the time it was returned to the earth as human manure. We were weak with laughter as the end approached.

One evening as she was leaping around with an imaginary scythe in her hand, reaping the wheat, my father walked in. The sight of her leg kicking the air delighted him. Suddenly nanny saw the master. I suppose it must have been like being seen in your underpants by the Pope. She sat down on the spot with her toe still in the air. We died with laughter.

Azra was a different case. She was not quite a slave, but almost. She had been hired for seven years for a lump sum. This contract was known as *ajir shodan* or long-term labour. Her parents had died. She had a needy brother who worked in the Bazaar and an older, slightly sinister sister, who earned her living by sewing in private houses and selling talismans. She never went anywhere without taking a small bundle in which she kept a shroud. She was called "Dokhtar-Agha", or Master's daughter. They were 'Seyeds'. Azra, her sister and her brother had dark, lean faces and huge black eyes. Like most of the Seyeds whom I have met, they had good diction. Azra was Mama's maid and did all that was required of her.

A mother and daughter team looked after Bishana. The mother, Zahra, was deaf and dumb. She worked hard for a small return, but could not communicate except with a few basic signs such as right hand to mouth, eating. Both hands to mouth, drinking from a bowl. Index dangling, a male person. Thumb between index and second finger, a female, and so on. Belghais, her fleshy and forward daughter, was not much use except that she possessed all her five senses and she could take orders and translate them to her mother in a strange sign language.

Medina, the Shahsavan, and another peasant woman called Laily did the rough work but were not really permanent.

From these and others who came and went, we learnt many things. For instance, we learnt that Isfahanis were the true Scottish Jews, famous for their tightfistedness, cleverness and industry. Azerbaijanis, on the other hand, were renowned for their stupidity, but they were brave. Not so the Kashanis, who were the true cowards. The Ghazvinis were distinguished by their sodomy and the Mazandaranis for their moral laxity.

We also learnt improper expressions. If a man was inordinately proud, he would address himself to his posterior and say "Pray, do not follow me. You stink." Or if he was old and decrepit, "A mouse could pull barley from his behind." But we soon learnt not to repeat these.

Chapter 18

THE LADY IN THE RED HAT

As I explained before, we lived on the north-west side of Tehran on the very edge of the town. Our property was bounded by two *kuchés* (or lanes) as yet without name. The one on the south was a short cul-de-sac; the one on the north was narrow but quite long. My grandmother's house faced the southern *kuché*; Papa's office, which had been the house of the rich merchant, and the guests' villa, faced the northern one, in which there were three houses. The rest was a stony waste. This was vaguely called a *kharabé* in Persian, meaning a ruin, although it does not mean that there had

52

been a building on the site before. It often meant desolate and un-cultivated land, and although land was extremely cheap and build-ing costs next to nothing, people did not have the urge to invest in property as yet. Homeless squatters often came and parked them-selves in one of these unenclosed spaces until they became a nuis-ance and were driven away. On one occasion, there was such an 'eyesore' opposite the guests' villa. A *hammal* (or coolie) had dug a hole in the ground and covered the entrance with dirty old sack-ing. It was rumoured that he lived there with his seven wives.

"How on earth can he afford seven," asked Papa, "while I can only afford one?"

"He doesn't keep them; they support him. They go out to work and take in washing."

"What with? There is no water in that hole."

It was really extraordinary how they existed. Piles of house-hold rubbish were dumped there every day. The stench and flies were quite disgusting, yet the pile was usually topped by one or two crawling heirs of the *hammal*.

On the other side, towards the end of our lane, someone had wired off a piece of land and was using it as a chicken market. This deterioration of the neighbourhood into slums worried Mama. She persuaded my father's friend and former secretary, a fat gentleman called Ezaz-el-mulk, to buy the *hammal's* derelict space and use the site to build a house for his family. And to insulate us from the chickens, Mama herself bought a piece of land beyond the stables for a song, and let it stand for a while. Before long they started building a house on it and we went to watch the building's progress every day while we were in Tehran. First, trenches were dug and then foundations built. Damp courses, as such, were not used in buildings and they sorted out the damp problem in the tra-ditional way by building a vaulted and ventilated basement under the house, but this building had no basement and sprang straight from the ground. The part we liked best was to watch bricks being thrown in the air by one man and caught in mid-air by another who was standing on the wall he was erecting. The bricklayer sang out his request for a brick with a monotonous but pleasant phrase. At a certain word, the man down below made a verbal response and immediately the brick was hurled into the air and caught with a graceful movement. We were told that this word was the signal that the man standing on the ground was about to throw the brick otherwise it would bounce back on his head. There were no drains and no wiring for electricity, and the whole business of building was very simple. But I remember lovely mouldings on the ceilings which were, unfortunately, not done when we were there to watch. We later learnt that the rooms were going to be painted in different pastel shades, which was currently fashionable. This house was meant to be occupied by my three brothers when they returned from Europe.

About this time I heard a very significant conversation. One day at lunch Mama suddenly asked my father, "Have you been seeing him?" He looked rather surprised and said, "As a matter of fact, we met two nights ago. We shook hands like strangers and talked about impersonal matters. But how do *you* know?"

"I guessed. This morning I had a visit from Madame M. She never visits anyone unless she thinks they are on the way up again. So I thought perhaps an attempt was being made at reconciliation."

Papa shrugged and changed the subject. "The Major asked me if I would consider letting the *bironi* (outer apartment) for a year to a very distinguished European whom he has recently met. He said it would involve putting in a European-style lavatory and bathroom upstairs. I said I would have to ask you."

"Why not? As you are away most of the time you no longer need an office." Mama was always on the side of economy.

One afternoon the distinguished European and his wife came to see the house. I had taken it on myself to clean out Papa's desk and was shaking a duster in the garden when I looked up and there they were. They smiled at me - at me, mind you - dusty little unkempt thing that I was. They were the most beautiful and civilised couple that I had ever seen. He was tall and handsome, dressed in a dark grey suit; and she looked incredibly beautiful. In her mid-twenties and slim, she had the air of someone entirely independent and free. Her oval face was framed by her light brown hair, on top of which was perched a little red hat. She was wearing a very smart navy blue suit and silk blouse. Her expensive shoes and handbag looked as though they were specially designed to go with her suit. When she smiled, I noticed that she had a dimple. Oh, how I wished I could be like her!

All the women I had known so far, either plain or pretty, had some flaw. They were either servile to their husbands, or pulled down by their children or other cares, but this one seemed carefree, and I imagined she would be able to walk into a king's palace without being stopped by a single sentry. In short, she made a very strong impact on me. Little was I to know how far she would be responsible for altering the course of our lives.

Their name was Lapidos and they became our first tenants.

Chapter 19

THE WALK

Amir-Monazam had given Papa two sensible pieces of advice: first, to settle new families in the village to work the land; second, to acquire and train a lot of dogs to "protect you against thieves and Arabs". He himself gave us a few of the latter to start with. As children we were not so interested in people as in dogs. These dogs were of various breeds - sheepdogs, Tazis or greyhounds, and the sturdy mongrel guard dog, the mainstay of Persian villages, were given to us as puppies, tied to the trees all day, and gradually trained for their respective duties.

In Persia, the ownership of many dogs did not indicate a man's wealth and influence. Dogs were considered unclean creatures which in theory a good Moslem should never touch and should be glad to be rid of. I love the story of the lazy mullah whose robe was once brushed by a passing dog. He lifted his arms to heaven and said, "Inshallah - God willing - that was a cat". The metamorphosis would have saved him the washing of his robe. Dogs were not licensed or immunised. If they showed signs of rabies, they were shot. The only places where they were tolerated were in the villages. There they protected the inhabitants against wild beasts and invaders. The dogs like their human counterparts had to exist on small sustenance; no vitamins or meat for these creatures. They lived on coarse barley bread when they could get it. They were hungry most of the time and, as intended, fierce. At night they were let loose and were welcome to eat any wild creature they tore apart, but if they stole domestic animals and birds they were shot.

When we first saw the puppies they were yelping. They were tied to trees near the garage and their piteous noise filled all our days and was most distressing. We wanted them freed, but were told that this could not be done as they were meant to become guard dogs and not lap dogs. We noticed that every time we came near they stopped their horrid yowls and jumped at us. At first we were nervous but we soon realised that they wanted to play and lick our hands. We brought them bowls of water and some yoghurt from the house. That went down very well. The puppies had a peculiar kind of fly on them, a squat, grey fly with suction feet. These we were told were *sag magas*, or dog flies, one of the crosses a dog had to bear although it didn't do them any harm.

We were wary of Fandogh, the large collie with black markings. It had the reputation of being the fiercest of them all. However, from the start, it was plain that there was one particular puppy which could not make a guard dog for anyone except for my sisters and for me. He rolled on his back every time we approached him and rubbed his ears on our feet. He was a large, yellow, hairy creature who, according to the farm manager, must have descended from a wasp. Persians are notoriously lazy at classifying plants and animals. To them any flower is *gol* and any dog a *sag*. But even so, I am sure that our new friend would have confounded any attempt at tracing his genealogy.

The funny thing was that the manager, Mohammad-Beg, the former coachman, being Turkish could not pronounce '*Zanbour*', the Persian word for a wasp and insisted on calling it '*Zanbouz*'. We were so delighted with this mispronunciation that the name stuck. Zanbouz was such a sloppy, irresistible character that he was soon released from captivity, and allocated to us as a bodyguard when we were old enough to walk out of our garden without an adult companion.

He never stopped following us except to bark at unseen, imaginary, attackers in the distance. He was one of the few dogs allowed inside the inner garden wall, but the house remained out of

56

bounds and he lay on the gravel underneath the veranda. When we wished to call him and he was nowhere in sight, we simply went into the kitchen and banged the chopper on the meat-board and he came running in, dribbling at the mouth. At night, however, he joined the pack and barked for his living.

One day our walk took us out of the drive at the end of which the *asiab*, or water-mill was situated. It was a prosperous and lively place. The miller who looked like the 'abominable snowman' greeted us with a dusty grin and his mate showed us into the inner mysteries of the mill. It was in a cool, stone-built basement without windows. The sound of the huge upper-stone rotating was deafening and, as in the case of the *tanur*, we were not allowed too near the works, but sat on a platform and watched the smooth flow of flour down a chute emptying into sacks, which the mate had to move when filled. My mother liked our flour to be twice milled which made for whiter bread, but the miller did not approve of this and assured us that coarse bread was good for one.

At the side of the mill was a huge black hole some eighteen feet in diameter and fifteen or twenty feet deep, at the bottom of which was a wooden water-wheel. A rushing stream forced its way through a narrow passage falling down through this hole for ever, with a great noise. On the narrowest part of the passage was built a bridge without parapets. We were told that if we fell into the water we would be carried down to the bottom of the hole, where we would not only be drowned but torn to shreds by the water-wheel. Oddly enough, there was no attempt to fix a grill in front of the hole. The mill served not only our village but also many neighbouring villages, which on occasions brought their wheat to Meshkin-Abad to be milled.

Because Meshkin-Abad was on the direct route from Karaj to a group of villages in Kharaquan, our village was never short of a caravan in transit. We often saw camels crouching in the marshy meadows near the mill. Rough-looking turbaned men lounged there, smoking and chatting, or making tea on smokey, tin samovars. Once the mill was in operation, it became a social centre for men who stopped on their way home and gossiped with strangers. At night, when the caravans resumed their journey, camel bells filled the distance with a harmonious sound and the cameleers' melancholic songs never struck a false note. When we were old enough to know, we realised that these men sang long and numerous poems of Hafiz and Saadi although they could not read or write.

However, to go back to our walk, having reached the mill, we now had the choice of three ways. One was to turn sharp right. This would have taken us by the cemetery at the edge of which ran a stream, lined by service trees. Here, for some reason that we could not fathom, the moss that covered the stones at the bottom of the stream was red. There was much superstition concerning this phenomenon as all water-moss elsewhere in the village was green. Past the cemetery the ground rose and, if we followed the stream, we eventually got to the gorge where the *ghanat* surfaced.

The left-hand track from the mill went dustily on and on and was very dull unless we bore right and climbed over some ruined walls in order to get to the *ghaleh*. For some reason we found the ruined walls rather frightening and so did not go that way.

Our favourite way was to cross the deadly bridge over the fast-running stream at the side of the mill. This took us over footpaths through some orchards (always rewarding in the summer) where we would stop in a meadow to look at a grey mare and foal, then cross the muddy stream in front of the *ghaleh*, and watch women making dung cakes. This was fascinating. Two women dipped their hands into piles of soaked cow dung and taking out handfuls, flattened them out on the ground into eight-inch discs and left them in the sun to dry. Funnily enough, they didn't smell too badly when dried out.

There were always the same two leathery women doing the job. They were ageless, skinny and austere, but not frightening. They never smiled at us, but they weren't hostile. They just ignored us as though we were irrelevant to their lives. Their detachment in some way reminded me of the beautiful lady in the red hat. She was desirable, free and gay. These poor souls were the exact opposite. It was like the similarity between salt and sugar.

We watched these women to our hearts' content and then we either came back the same way, or jumped over the narrowest part of the stream, where Zanbouz led, and came back by way of the cemetery.

58

Author's father in Cossack uniform on his wedding night.

Amir Monazam and Papa.

Pari, Zarin and Maryam.

My uncle, the Mirpange.

A journey to Meshkin-Abad.

Papa and Jamshid in Meshkin-Abad.

Reza Shah with his Generals. The author's father is second from left.

*From left to right: Reza Khan, Ahmad Shad Ghazar and the author's father
in Isfahan.*

Chapter 20

LOVE

The greatest advantage of the move to Meshkin-Abad, as far as we were concerned, was the ending of the nightmare lessons and our release from the tyranny of the mad mullah.

Now it was felt that we were due for further instruction and Papa took it upon himself to teach us. He had no previous experience of teaching and no theories about it. Apart from an Arabic copy of the Koran, there were only three books in the village, 'The Golestan' of Saadi, the poems of Hafiz and a Persian translation of *Gil Blas* which Mama was reading at the moment. 'Golestan' was the obvious choice. The only way I can describe the main work of the great poet is as a collection of philosophical and moral stories interspersed with poems. Saadi's prose, as well as his poems, is valued for its inspired simplicity. The clarity of his language, after seven hundred years of invasion and convulsions in the life of the nation, is such that any child can read and understand it, at least partially. Anway, there was no other choice. So we had one hour's daily diet of Saadi without tears.

Papa asked each of us to read aloud for twenty minutes at each lesson while the other two listened. He corrected our mistakes as we went along but left out the Arabic quotations and long words which we could not grasp, saying that we would have to go over the book again when we had learnt to read fluently. He insisted, however, that we should learn all the poems in each lesson by heart. Those who did received a boiled sweet at the end of the lesson, but for those who did not, there was no punishment. As we got older, the sweets ceased but there was talk of competition with my brothers and a prize.

After the lessons came sewing, which we found exceedingly tedious. Mama had rugs spread on the western veranda which was pretty shady till about noon where she was busy sewing endless sheets and mosquito nets on a small Singer sewing machine. If it wasn't that, it was dull clothes for the servants. We had to learn tacking, stitching and picking. To the question "What happens if the children stitch their fingers in the sewing machine?", Mama replied dryly, "They'll do it only once". Sewing went on till lunch which never seemed too early.

One day, while we were sewing, a message arrived from the Karaj Garrison that the Major and Monsieur Lapidos (our tenant) would arrive that evening. Mama was very pleased. She ordered chickens to be killed, marrows and aubergines to be picked, and rice to be soaked in salt water for pilau. When Ismail heard the news, he told us that Europeans always eat salad with their meals. He had masses of tomatoes and cucumber sliced and, for want of anything better, poured on it some of the unrefined olive oil which was used for cleaning Mama's patent leather shoes, and some vinegar. We also felt slightly embarrassed about the absence of European-style lavatories. Both of ours were found wanting. Papa's, a small, dark cubicle, had two uncompromising bats fluttering about it; and the other, a large desolate place, was used by the servants, and they had, a few days before, reported that a snake was seen hanging down from the ceiling.

In the late afternoon, the party arrived in Lapidos's swanky sports car. To our dismay, the gorgeous lady was not with them, but it later turned out to be just as well. After greeting the guests, Mama said to the Major, "I hope you have brought me some letters from my sons?" When he replied that none had arrived yet, her face fell and she was not very jolly during the rest of that evening. I noticed the segregation of the sexes was never observed when we were in the village. We all ate with the male guests. For our part, we were absolutely hypnotised by the six-foot-tall European with his deep blue eyes. We followed him everywhere and were treated kindly and gently by him as though we were not the urchins we were, but something special. It was the first time in our lives that a man had stepped back for us to precede him. At dinner he was polite and attentive to my mother and to us, and later opened a large box of chocolates and let us eat as many as we could manage. After dinner, we sat on the veranda and played records on a hand-

60

operated gramophone. He went to his car and produced some huge records the size of which we had never seen before. They had red centres on which there was a picture of a dog. The music was unfamiliar, but very rousing. At this point, I was terribly in love. He was so great and magnificent - no wonder the perfect lady had agreed to be his wife.

For the first time I was made conscious of my appearance. I had a hasty look in my mother's mirror. Oh, dear! What a terrifying sight met my eyes. How could I hope to compete with the red-hatted lady? My hair was long, stringy and dead straight; however my eyebrows were curly. My beady black eyes didn't help much, and my large nose made it worse. I reassured myself that I had a good nature and an easy smile, but that was not enough. I must have some beauty to go with it. Mother's room was in semi-darkness as all the oil lamps had been taken out to light the veranda. With a blunt pair of scissors I cut off some of my eyebrows, making a botched job of it.

Before going to bed, I dampened my hair, rolled it up in bits of twigs and tied it securely with some white cotton which I took off the sewing machine. I also scraped some chalk off the walls in case my colour should need lightening up next day. I was going to be dazzlingly beautiful. Perhaps not as smart as the lady in the red hat, but equally composed. It was a pity I was so young - perhaps once I was made up, I would look a little older.

I could hardly sleep that night as a result of being over-tired; also, a couple of mosquitoes had crept under my net and were pestering me. The next morning I overslept. I was shaken rudely awake by Medina, who said: "Wake up! Breakfast is nearly over!" I jumped up and suddenly remembering the rollers, I dashed towards the stream hoping to get them out without being seen. As I had no mirror to guide me, it was extremely difficult to disentangle the cotton from the twigs; the more I tugged at them the tighter they became. I was there for a long time. Eventually, I heard someone shouting, "Is she coming? Or shall I clear the breakfast table?" Medina replied, "I don't know. The one who never washes cannot leave the water alone this morning."

At last I removed the twigs with a handful of my hair, the remainder had fuzzed up like that of a negress. When I passed my mother's mirror, I nearly had a fit. On top of that misfortune, I had been bitten by a mosquito on my nose and upper lip. I truly looked a sight.

When I got to the dining-room, the guests were leaving and I gathered they were going back to the town. Rather than dazzle everyone with my beauty I crept behind the door and waited for the car to start. Later on, one of my sisters remarked, "Pari does look odd today". Mama replied absently, "Perhaps she slept too much. That makes you puffy, you know."

Chapter 21

IZRAIL DEFIED

Papa was playing the part of Dr. Livingstone now, although he had never heard of the good doctor. He was determined to root out malaria from the village. He got men to drain all the waterlogged areas. He impressed on the villagers the need to keep their families (especially the babies of whom there was a crop each year, but few of whom survived) inside mosquito nets when they had to sleep out of doors. He showed them a picture of the offending mosquito and told them that it was much more harmful than a snake, and responsible for the deaths of their infants. I don't think many of them believed this, as the idea of 'Az-Ma-Behtaran' (malevolent spirits) was firmly embedded in their minds. We spent the afternoons filling empty capsules with the bitter white powder of quinine. These were freely distributed among the peasants who called for them at the house as soon as they felt ill, no matter what the symptoms. We had to take sugar-coated pills which we had learnt from experience not to suck.

Then it happened that my sister, Maryam, was struck down. Within twenty-four hours, she had developed a high temperature and was delirious. Her teeth were clenched and nothing could be got down her throat; and her pupils became fixed. Village women who saw her said that their own children had gone through the same stages before the end came.

Mama was desperate. She could not move the child to Tehran at that point and there was no hope of receiving proper medical help in that isolated place. She prayed and she allowed her women to carry out remedial magic to remove the 'evil eye'. This was done by writing with a piece of charocal on an egg the names of all those who had seen the child in the last seven days. If there was no one present who could write, faces were drawn and a few magic symbols were added. Then the egg was circled round the child's head and the names chanted out. At the mention of each name, the woman holding the egg gave a slight pressure to the ends with her thumb and forefinger. At whosoever's name the egg broke, it meant that that person had caused the 'evil eye'. But this did not indicate evil intention. Indeed, it could be that the child's own mother was responsible for the evil eye for some reason, such as having too much pride in her offspring, and causing envy among the mysterious forces that regulate our fate. The breaking of the egg simply broke the charm and that was that. I never discovered whether Mama really believed in magic. She certainly always spoke against love potions and destructive magic. However, this was neither the time nor place to make such enquiries.

Papa, having sent the car and the driver with an urgent request for a doctor to the Garrison Commander in Karaj hours before, paced the length of the veranda, helplessly muttering to himself.

Mama was moaning inside the sick room while the women were speculating outside the door as to whether the girl would be buried in the village cemetery or taken to Tehran and laid among the family group.

Hours seemed to pass. The midday sun beat down on the great stillness. No meals were served. Zari and I were beginning to cry, intensely aware of our mother's abject misery. First, she had not heard from her sons in the distant lands for months, and now poor Maryam was as good as dead. As a last desperate act, she had asked Jamshid and Ismail to run all the three miles to Ghale Nou and ask Amir-Monazam to come - for what reason, she did not know.

Now we were like ancient mariners on a windless sea. Nothing moved, nothing happened, nor could it. Suddenly we heard dogs barking and then a car. We rushed to the gate and saw Amir-Monazam's car racing towards the house. With him were Ismail, Jamshid and another, a middle-aged man.

The sight of the angels in paradise would not have pleased my parents more than the sight of Doctor Amir Khan, who had come to spend the weekend with his friend, Amir-Monazam.

The doctor examined Maryam. One of the village women shouted, "Too late! She is dead!" He paid no heed, and out of his bag he took a syringe and injected a strong dose of quinine into her thigh. The villagers present spread the word that the doctor had to stick a needle into the child to find out whether she was dead or alive. They themselves could tell such things by the signs.

They came the following day and were surprised to see that my sister was still alive. The doctor also called and gave Maryam another injection. He told my parents to take her to Tehran for further treatment as soon as she was well enough to travel. The village began to talk of a miracle. The dead child had been brought back to life - by a needle? Not on your life.

Chapter 22

EXPOSURE

I was having tea with my mother when we first heard of the catastrophe without learning the details.

Tea in Persia is not accompanied by scones, cakes, best china and silver teapots. Nor is it a question of everyone sitting at the table and drinking at the same time. It is a most informal meal. The only person who has to be there at all times is the *abdar bashi*, or the pourer from the samovar. Others come and go between 3 and 5 p.m. Nothing is eaten except at receptions. Tea is poured into small glasses, with or without lemon, and conversation is not compulsory.

Usually, when we were in town, the pourer was the younger nanny, Dayé. She was cheerful and chatted easily. On this occasion, for some reason, Mama was pouring and I was the only customer. Then my father came in, looking most upset. Mother said "I see you have come to tell me the worst. Please proceed."

She had for some time been convinced that some terrible misfortune must have happened to my brothers in Europe. There had been no word from them for a long time. Mama had sent several letters which the Major (the only person in the family who could write French) had addressed and posted himself. He said he could not understand it, and suggested that perhaps the boys had changed their address. Papa had contacted the Ministry of Foreign Affairs and asked them to make enquiries at our Embassy in Paris to find out whether his sons were all right. Mama was convinced that at least one of her sons must be dead and the tragedy was being concealed from her. She had braced herself for the worst.

Papa replied: "Yes, it is very bad news, but it does not concern our sons. The Major is in trouble, He is about to be arrested, and has begged me to take him to Meshkin-Abad tonight, otherwise he threatens to blow his brains out."

"Oh, dear! What is it? Another political conspiracy to discredit you?"

Papa wasn't sure. He said that his nephew had refused to speak, but promised to explain everything once they got to Meshkin-Abad.

That was that. The chauffeur was quickly found and the two were off.

Presently, Mama's brother, the *mirpange*, called and soon after that, the Major's mother, a dear, devout lady, who was my aunt, appeared in great distress. She wanted to see her son to hear what had happened, but he was not there. Everyone felt sorry for her as she had recently lost a brave son in battle, and now it seemed that her other beloved son, the Major was in trouble. No one seemed to know why and everyone was bewildered.

During intervals that night, there were knocks on the doors of the house. At first the gendarmes were sent away good-naturedly. Then they grew tough and threatened to break in and look for their man, but they had no warrant and would not say what they wanted him for. At last Mama had to see their officer and explain that their man was in Meshkin-Abad.

Papa came back the next day in a most dejected mood. He was full of bitterness and scorn.

"The fool," he said, "has embezzled several thousand *tomans* of Army Treasury funds and has been found out. He was led to believe by the Lapidoses that the money would be invested in a lucrative project that would bring one hundred per cent profit in a short time so that he could replace it before it was missed."

"Why couldn't he have put it back when he first realised he was suspected?"

"Because he hasn't got it. The fool says he gave it all to Lapidos."

"I don't understand. Why couldn't Lapidos be made to return the money?"

"Because he gave it to his wife who has disappeared to Europe without a trace."

"That explains why the gendarmes were so keen to search the apartment of the foreigner."

"Did they find him?"

"No. His servant said that he was at an hotel."

"They will get him."

The months that followed were the most dismal in the history of my family. The nastiness of this affair affected us all, particularly my father, who felt thoroughly betrayed. He had served his country conscientiously and had never accepted a bribe, hoping to die with a clean record. Now for the first time in his life, he felt ashamed before other men. He shunned society and was most depressed.

The inquiry dragged on for months during which it was revealed that Lapidos and his wife were international confidence tricksters, who had worked their way to Tehran where they 'hit the jackpot' in the person of the poor, simple Major. How they persuaded him to take such a grave step was never revealed, but I should not think it was very difficult.

This episode, apart from the public disgrace, did much personal damage to my parents. To begin with, during the inquiry,

66

the Major claimed ownership of the new house that had just been finished. To prove this, he produced receipts from builders made out to him personally. The house was to be confiscated, and its value set against his liabilities. In fact, the house belonged to Mama; she had only asked him to supervise its building as she herself was away in Meshkin-Abad. My parents kept the worthless deeds of the house till the end of their lives. The Army, anxious to recover some of its losses, sent bailiffs to seize the house, and Papa felt too miserable at the time to contest this. Also, he was reluctant to hurt my aunt hoping that the confiscation of the property might reduce the punishment of her misguided son.

The final and most cruel blow was the revelation that my brothers had received no news of the family for six months and had had no money sent to them. They were bewildered and penniless.

My brothers, Ali, Nosrat and Vali, had been sent by the Army to France for their education where they only received a grant for their university fees, their personal expenses being paid by Papa who, at the beginning of every month, gave the Major a draft to transfer to France. Being at the Treasury, it was a very easy matter for him.

It now appeared that the Major had put the money into his own account and destroyed all my brothers' letters. This Mama never forgave.

The worse of it was that it was a family scandal - not a case of a hired secretary whom you could denounce and disown. Papa had to think of his sister's distress, Mama's agony, and the poor young man himself who, through his senseless crime, had harmed everyone and not even benefited himself.

Eventually, the Major was court-martialled, lost his rank and all civil rights for life, and was sentenced to fifteen years in jail. Lapidos was tried by a civil court, and my poor beloved received twenty years' hard labour.

Chapter 23

POETRY

For some months after the affair, Papa felt as though he had been stained by something nasty, and could not bring himself to join the society of his friends and former colleagues. He became a recluse and delved more and more deeply into himself and his new-found interests. He planted a large peach orchard and cultivated many varieties of peaches and nectarines. He resurrected old vine-yards and made new ones, and got specialists to show him how to prune and how to treat the soil. The vineyards were not for the purpose of wine-making but for dessert grapes. These were the common varieties of Yaghouti, Asgari and Muscatel grapes.

Grapes have many uses in Persia. For instance, some grapes are picked unripe and the juice pressed out to make unfermented vinegar, called *abghure*. This has an excellent flavour and is an essential part of Persian cooking.

The pressing operation lasts all day and as we had no mechanical press we got a young man to tread the grapes in a vat. Before he did this, he was sent to have a bath, then had to wash his feet again. Unfortunately, it was overlooked that this particular young man suffered from syphilis, but no one was the worse for this contagion. After a day of treading, he was fed on honey and the so-called "hot" food to counterbalance the "cold" sucked into his system through trampling the acid grapes. *Shireh* or syrup of grapes was another useful produce and widely used as a substitute for sugar. Vine leaves made delicious *dolme*, stuffed with meat and herbs, while raisins and sultanas were a major calorie-producing food in winter.

But Papa had another use for grapes. This was the production of arak, the brother of vodka. The material for this had been fermenting in the *borj* for some time. Now it was taken out and

68

emptied into a *deeg* and subjected to the same sort of treatment as Mama's rose water, except that it had to be more carefully distilled. Papa kept on taking samples and measuring the alcohol content with a special gadget, and letting the flow run out until he was satisfied with the results. Then he collected the distillation in a large jug, redistilled it, corked it and put it away. He did all this by himself and did not ask the women to help him as they would not understand the chemistry of the juice and might spoil it. Incidentally, distillation of spirit was not yet illegal or a Government monopoly. All drinks were made at home. Papa filled fifty-seven bottles. Mama complained that it was too much. He replied that her own brother, the *mirpange*, made five dozen of *each flavour*.

Meanwhile, our education was pursued with the utmost energy. My father produced two more books to broaden our minds. One was a book of Persian Poets and the other, a history of Persia.

From the book of the poets we learnt how Manouchehri had painted a picture of words from scenes of changing seasons; how Ferdosi quarrelled with King Sultan Mahmud Ghaznavi, and how he debunked him with poems. Hafiz burnt like a wax candle throughout, and his feet never touched the ground. On the other hand, how Saadi's feet sometimes dragged, having lived one hundred and twenty years, and travelled the world for a quarter of that time; how when he was travelling near Jerusalem, he was captured by Christian Crusaders and sent to work in the clay pits of Tripoli beside Jews "and other strays", and how a friend from Allepo, passing through this city by chance, heard of his predicament and "bought" the greatest poet of the age for ten gold pieces, took him back to Allepo and gave him his own daughter for a wife. The bride, it appeared, was of such a nasty temper that after a while Saadi began to feel that he had exchanged one prison for another. All this was to help us to understand the stories behind the poems, although many of the poems themselves we did not understand, having memorised them by their sound.

After supper we sat round a metal stove and began our *mosh-aéré*, or poetry competition, in which Papa acted as referee. He had all the prizes put out - bowlfuls of pistachio nuts, roasted chickpeas mixed with sultanas; all to be won by those who scored most points.

Moshaéré, I always think, is a kind of mental tennis. You send a volley correctly into the opponent's court, but so aimed as to make it difficult to return, whilst being ready to hit any awkward balls which might bounce back into your own court. It is, in fact, a precise contest with many rules, but in our case, the rules were relaxed. We were allowed to quote one, two, three or four lines of any poem enough to make sense, but we had to choose our poems so that the first letter was the same as the last letter of the preceding poem. For example, if your poem ended with "D", whoever came after should start his with "D", and so on.

In every language there are some letters which do not occur very frequently at the beginning of the words, such as "X" and "Z" in English. In Persian "L", for instance, is common at the end of words but uncommon at the beginning. In order to have every one tied into a knot, you had to memorise a whole *ghazal* (long poem) ending with "L"; and in order not to be tied up yourself (in case one of the other contestants had the same idea), you searched through books and found enough lines to fire back. Papa disqualified any poem which was not authentic, and opened the contest himself by quoting the following verse of Saadi:

> A tablet of perfumed clay one day in the bathhouse
> Came from the hand of an attendant to mine
> I asked it, "are you musk or are you amber,
> That I am drunk with your lovely perfume?"
> Said the clay, "I was only humble mud
> But I sat for a while with flowers.
> You smell the perfection of my companions
> Otherwise I am the mud that I am."

"Give me 'M'," said Papa.

> My love for black eyes is deeply embedded
> To this destiny I am much indebted.

"Give me a 'D',"

> During prayers when the arch of your eyebrows
>   came to memory,

70

I was so moved that the altar groaned.

"Give me a 'D'."

> Dear friend is the one who holds out a hand,
> In misery and bewilderment.

"Give me a 'T'."

> Thou has gone and broken thy faith . . .

At this point we all called out "Pyjama Cord". "Pyjama Cord" or "*Bande Tonbuni*" is an expression used for strung or improvised, in short, incorrect poems. Papa upheld the objection. Sometimes when Ismail got to a particularly rousing passage of the Shahnamé martial poems, he went over the four-line limit and we listened spellbound, as it sounded so good. He stopped when he ran out of breath, or found a suitably difficult ending to stop at.

Outside a jackal howled. Dogs stampeded and barked in unison. The ancient pear tree, after producing half a ton of the most delectable fruit in her advanced years, heaved in the autumn wind like a ship in heavy seas.

Inside the dimly lit room, flowers talked, nightingales wept; the love-stricken moth burned her wings in the flames of the eternal candle, and the whole range of human fantasy was woven into a strange tapestry of words.

Chapter 24

TRAVELLERS' RETURN

Our cat, 'Princess' entertained us in a different way this morning: she caught a large snake, smashed its head, and yawling, brought it indoors, and then circled the mosquito net that Maryam and I shared, with the dead reptile dangling in her mouth. And that is how we woke up that Friday morning.

'Princess', a pure white cat with one blue and one green eye, was most enterprising and used to catch all sorts of large and small creatures. At night, she and her fat, black husband, called 'Agha', or 'Sir', used to sit at the foot of the table and watch us having our evening meal. Sometimes Papa threw a tasty morsel to 'Princess', but 'Sir', with typical male lack of conscience, snatched it in mid-air and ate it. Then 'Princess' stretched a long, graceful paw and hit him gently on the head. At this rebuke, the dignified 'Agha' took umbrage and turned his back on his wife. We loved to watch this game, with the result that the cats never stopped begging.

'Princess' had several kittens with 'Agha'. They were all pure white and had odd eyes. I sometimes used to smuggle one of the kittens to bed. At first it would purr and then fall silent. I, frightened lest it was suffocated, would give it a pinch, whereupon it would yell and I would be discovered.

As I said, this was Friday. Fridays were usually "good" days. There was plenty of good food and sometimes quite a bit of excitement. Every Thursday evening, the muleteer was sent to Karaj with two donkeys to buy provisions. The car was rarely used for this purpose as the track was still rough, and spare parts expensive. The main item of shopping was a load of ice brought down from the mountains, meat, paraffin, small items of farm machinery and seeds.

Friday's feast consisted of *chelo-kabab*, a dish of rice and meat. Rice was boiled in salted water, then cooked in butter for a

72

length of time. Meanwhile, the meat, which had been cut into cubes and flavoured with onion, was pierced by long skewers and barbecued on charcoal. When all was ready, the rice was heaped onto plates and the roast meat put in the centre. On this went the yolk of an egg, a pat of butter and powdered *sumac*, a reddish powder with a divine flavour. I never forgot an Englishman's remark about it. He said that if we compare marriage to a wholesome meal like *chelo-kabab*, one of its components, love, is like *sumac*, assuredly the best part, but by itself, alas, quite unsatisfactory. With this meal one drank *doogh* (watered down yoghurt), which was bottled, tightly corked, and left under a small waterfall to become cool and gaseous.

After lunch came the most exciting part of Friday, making ice cream. This operation was entirely carried out by the children, with Jamshid in charge. We carefully mixed our egg yolks, cream, milk, sugar and vanilla together, poured it into the inner cylinder of the churn which was then placed inside the wooden casing and the space between packed with ice. It was then only a matter of two hours' hard churning before any result showed. We made so much noise that no one got a siesta on Friday. Whoever did the most churning had the first bowlful of ice cream when it was ready. Sometimes it was disappointing, like the time when some salt got into the cylinder and gave its contents a peculiar flavour. Once or twice the liquid refused to congeal, no matter how much it was churned, and we ended up by drinking it. But it was great fun and I think that it made the grown-ups happy to see us enjoy ourselves.

This particular Friday, however, was doubly exciting as we were awaiting my brothers' arrival from Europe. Abbas had taken the car to Tehran to meet them and drive them to Meshkin-Abad as soon as they arrived from Bandar-Pahlavi, which was where their latest telegram had come from. Lunch had been served an hour late in the hope that they might be in time to partake of it. Jamshid held the ice cream back for half an hour before he declared that it must be eaten then or never.

The shadows were getting longer and we were tired of looking at the garden gate and listening for the sound of an approaching car. So I went into the house and began dressing my rag doll with a bundle of clothes that Nanny had made for it. Stuck to the bundle was a threaded needle and a prized possession, a safety pin. I kept holding these with my lips in order to have both hands free to dress the doll. Suddenly, the dogs barked and everyone rushed out with excitement. I was about to follow when I noticed that the safety pin was not there. I shook all my belongings and still couldn't find it. Surely I couldn't have swallowed it? By this time a great deal of noise was coming from the veranda. I looked out and there they were, two good-looking strangers, one tall, one short, in European clothes, and holding their hats. I was told they were my brothers Ali and Vali. The middle one, Nosrat, still had a few months of his studies to complete.

They picked me up and kissed me on my cheeks. My first words to them were: "I have just eaten a safety pin."

"Oh, dear! Was it open or closed?"

"Which is worse?"

"Open."

"I expect it was open."

My mother was determined that my metallic meal should not spoil this happy occasion. Delicious food was prepared for supper and the grown-ups talked and talked. My parents looked as happy as they had done before the Major's arrest. His name came up again and again, but was quickly dropped.

Ali, the eldest, who was already being called 'Captain' by the servants, asked how old I was.

"I don't know," I replied.

Mama came to the rescue and said, "She is eight and a quarter now."

"What do you mean, you don't know?" Ali said to me. "Can't you count?"

"No."

"Don't you go to school?"

"No."

"Oh, dear! That must be put right. Tomorrow I will take you to Tehran, have your silly long hair cut, buy you some pretty clothes, and find a school for you - for all three of you."

What a delightful prospect that seemed.

The next day, I did go to Tehran with my brothers, who had to report their arrival to the War Ministry, and receive instructions

74

as to their future work as Army Officers. I did not visit the hair-dressers though, or the shops. The purpose of my journey was to visit the family doctor and decide the fate of the safety pin within me.

He gave me a bottle of horrid oil to take several times a day and asked to be telephoned immediately if I experienced any pain. I went to stay in Nanny's little old-fashioned house with her charming family. Her kind daughter-in-law always smelt of fresh flowers and made me a necklace of white jasmine. Nanny took me out and bought me all sorts of little things that I fancied. However, I refused to cheer up. Autumn was drawing near and although the future promised to be happy with school and all that, I fancied that I might not be there to enjoy it. Nanny tried even harder to please me. She invited two large, loutish girls to come and play with me, but I didn't like them, so she took me out and bought me more toys.

At the end of the three days, a telegram came from my family, which read, "Safety pin found. Please return child."

Chapter 25

THE CHOICE

"The American Mission School is run by the Protestant missionaries in the same way as the Joan of Arc School is run by the Catholic Jesuits. They are primarily concerned with converting Persian girls to their respective religions," said my uncle.

"And whores," spat Lady Bride.

"What was that?" inquired Bishana, who was deaf.

"Whores, whores," boomed Lady Bride.

There was a distinct moment of embarrassment, not so much for slandering those worthy institutions as for uttering nasty words in the presence of the children. My mother blushed slightly, but

Lady Bride, her aunt by marriage, did not care. She had the physique of a retired wrestler attached to a viper's tongue. It was not easy to put her down.

The gathering was in Granny's room; my uncle was sitting on the only chair whilst the women sat cross-legged round Granny's bed which was spread on the floor. Mama had introduced the subject of school in order to pick the company's brains. Girls' schools were few and such a novelty in Iran. Now she was on the defensive.

"The General," she said, trying to invoke her husband's authority, "is also considering the Zoroastrian School."

"The Zoroastrians are entirely different in their attitude to religion," said my uncle approvingly. "They never try to convert anyone. In fact they would not take your soul if you offered it to them on a plate."

"Just as well!" burst out Lady Bride. "Who wants to join those sour-faced infidels?" She laughed a hearty belly laugh in which we all joined. Encouraged by this, she rasped, "In my younger days Jews and Gabres lived in their special quarters, wore long funny hats and were not allowed out of doors on rainy days in case water splashed their untouchable bodies and bounced back defiling the faithful. Now they live in our midst and there is no way of avoiding pollution. You can't even identify them."

My uncle suddenly appeared very stern. He moved his chair round until he came face to face with Lady Bride.

"The Zoroastrians, whom you slightingly call 'Gabres', are the most ancient inhabitants of Iran. Your ancestors, in fact, and mine. They are an honourable minority. So are the Jews and it is high time we stopped treating these people like dogs," he said with indignation.

* * *

My first day at school will always be associated with neighing horses.

It was early September and still too hot to walk. A *droshky* was brought to the door. My mother, Azra and we three girls got in. The driver put his foot nimbly on a ledge and climbed on to his high seat. He got hold of the reins and was about to order the horses on when one of them lifted his huge head and, baring his teeth like a dragon, let out a most terrifying neigh. It flashed across my mind that he could easily turn his head, pick me up and cut me into cubes fit for a barbecue. Or perhaps bolt and tear round the city until, as one sometimes hears it said, our "guts hung from Neghareh Khane" (the highest gallery in Tehran from which *neghare*, a musical instrument, was played at sunset). I put my foot on the running board and jumped off. My mother shouted in alarm and stopped the driver. He turned round and, seeing me in the road, was disgusted.

"What a stupid thing to do! You could have broken your leg," he spurted in a Turkish accent.

Mama said, "Get in, child. We will be late."

"I won't. The horse is going to bolt."

"Don't be silly, Miss. He won't bolt while I am in charge," said the driver, pointing to his wide person.

"Then stop him neighing."

As though to pacify me, the horse stopped at once. I got back into the carriage, shaking and apprehensive, hardly able to heed Mama's words. "If you should be asked for your surname, can you remember it?"

The name sounded unfamiliar. There had been no occasion for a surname before. We repeated it after her. The sound of our young voices reminded the horse of something and he neighed - no shrieked - with all his might. I whimpered. It was no use. I screamed and threatened to jump out if the man couldn't quieten the horse.

"Perhaps the child doesn't like the idea of going to school," said the Turkish fellow scornfully - not knowing how much I had looked forward to this occasion.

I had never seen a girls' school, or even passed in front of one. None of my girl cousins went to school and I didn't have a clue what to expect. But I reasoned it couldn't be very different from our classes in Meshkin-Abad, sitting under a shady tree and being taught by someone like Papa. There would be my sisters, of course, and perhaps two or three other girls - could they be our cousins Ghamar and Ghodsi?

We stopped in front of a large double-doored green gate which was padlocked. A small door had been set into one of the panels. We knocked on this and it was opened by a pink-cheeked, plump woman. After greeting us, she said, "My name is Gol (Flower). I am the caretaker's wife. Please come in and wait inside. I'll tell the headmistress you are here."

"Inside" was a funny kind of place - like the entrance to a maze. A curved wall separated the unroofed enclosure from the large, paved courtyard from which an ear-splitting din was emerging. We peeped through the narrow opening and saw numerous big and small brutish girls playing at a variety of games and shouting.

Azra hinted that we had come to the wrong address; this was perhaps a "hospital" by which she meant a lunatic asylum.

Suddenly a loud bell sounded. The girls stopped in the middle of hopping with one leg in the air and rushed to the centre of the yard where they formed a queue, two deep, holding hands. They waited some two minutes while stragglers joined them from all corners, running and grinning. Then a small woman with a frown rang a handbell. The girls ascended a short flight of stairs into a gallery and from there into the classrooms.

Gol returned to say that the headmistress would see us.

Nothing could be further from the "sour-faced Gabre" than Khanum Samieeyan, a young woman in her late twenties. She had short, curly hair and a good complexion, was tall, authoritative and very polite. (Recently I learnt that she was descended from Mirza Abdul Hassan Khan, the first Persian Ambassador to Great Britain (1809-10), whose diary was published in English in 1988). After we registered she explained that the school was in its infancy and had only six classes, but with an enlightened owner like Arbab-Kaykhosro Shahrukh the school was bound to expand and have a bright future. My mother said that our father's high regard for Arbab-Kaykhosro was one of the considerations for choosing that school, the other being the short distance from our house. Then the head asked if my father was a Bakhtiari chieftain.

"No, alas," replied my mother. "We belong to a lost tribe." This was treated as a joke.

It was agreed that we should be given a preliminary academic test while mother left for a morning's shopping.

We were examined for reading and given dictation at a slow pace - quite easy. Then followed a charade. We were asked to sit on seats placed well apart and given long sheets of paper. The examiner then said, "Write this down. My father grew eighteen *mans* (old unit of weight equal to three kilos) of grapes. He sold six *mans* for four *shahis* each (*shahi* was part of old Persian currency discontinued in the nineteen thirties). The next six *mans*, not so fresh now, he sold for three *shahis* each and he had to throw the rest away. How much money did he get?"

I was about to ask why the grapes were allowed to go bad when another problem was propounded.

"Hassan bought three pencils, four rubbers and a bag of eleven apples, and five handkerchiefs. How many objects did he buy?"

We stared blankly at the fat little dark woman who had posed these crazy questions, expecting explanations. None came. Instead she sat down pretending to be deaf and dumb.

What was one to write? How did they know that my father grew grapes? Perhaps Mama had mentioned it. But did he sell them at four *shahis* per *man*, and did he really have such wastage! How was I supposed to know about my father's transactions? I wrote, "My father does not sell his grapes."

The second question was not even worth worrying about. How could one buy clothes, food and stationery from the same shop? And what on earth was rubber? Was it liquid or solid? It was all very confusing. I left the question unanswered.

When mother came to collect us at noon, she was told that whereas our literary attainment was adequate for our age, we knew absolutely nothing about arithmetic. Therefore, it was decided that Zari and I should start in the second form and my sister, Maryam, in the beginners or first form.

At lunch I asked mother why she had told the teachers that Papa grew grapes. She couldn't understand what I was talking about.

I persisted. "He sold the first lot for four *shahis*, the second for three and the rest went bad." My parents and my brothers were listening to me now.

"What was your answer?" came the chorus.

"I wrote that my father does not sell his grapes."

Jamshid hooted with laughter and choked on his mouthful of

rice. In between coughs he kept repeating "does not sell his grapes".

Afterwards when I stopped being cross with him, Jamshid said, "I gather the school was not all that you expected?"

"No."

"There was no garden?"

"Not one green blade of grass."

"But the gate was green." (*'dare baghe sabz'*, or the 'green garden gate' is a term used for deception, meaning that the gate is green and not necessarily the garden.)

"So it was."

Chapter 26

HAMMAM

Bathing was a fascinating and terrifying experience. In Persia it is an ancient ritual, perhaps pre-Roman, and adapted to suit the needs of a Moslem society. Personal cleanliness was not only Godliness, but obligatory for all adult Moslems. A Moslem prays five times a day, but for the sake of convenience this was condensed into three daily sessions. Your daily prayers were not valid unless you had washed your hands, face and feet and it was a sacrilege to pray if you omitted to wash yourself after a bodily function.

There were various rules for ablutions (applicable to adults only), for submerging in a quantity of water (called *kor*) in all manner of circumstances quite incomprehensible to us, as they had Arabic names and were tactfully left out.

Normally one day a week was set aside for bathing. Each district had its own public bath given to it as a collective endowment or built by a rich grandee and named after him. These baths were perpetually heated and open to the public every day at a nominal charge.

Some of them represented feats of civil architecture and a few were lavishly decorated with hand-painted tiles and mosaics. I

80

always liked the story of the great genius of Isfahan who designed and built a great and beautiful bath which was entirely heated with a *pisuz* (fat-burning lamp). This was the object of much curiosity, so much so that an inquisitive builder tried to find out the secrets of its construction by digging at its foundation, thereby removing the lamp. Once that was done they could never get the bath to heat again.

Going back to our bathing - our mother, who could and did put up with much, could not stand public baths. She was determined that as soon as circumstances allowed, she would have her own bath built. As I mentioned in a former chapter, she had a bathhouse built on the far corner of the garden of the guest villa.

The bath had clumsy clanging iron doors specially made for it. The first led from the garden into the foyer where there was a platform for dressing and a small stone pool for dipping feet. There were two other iron doors in the foyer; one led into a small lavatory, which had been added since the Amir-Afshar episode, and the other opened into the bath. This consisted of an area of about ten yards by eight, divided into two parts, one for the steam and the other for the water. The steam part, covered in reddish-brown octagonal tiles half way up the walls, was used for sitting and washing. On the north wall there were two small leaded windows, as in a church. Sections of these could be opened to let out steam. On the south side there were two large basins side by side, seven feet by seven and eight feet deep. One contained cold water and the other hot. They were separated from one another and also from the rest of the *hammam* by a low stone parapet. These basins were called *khazineh* and had a steep flight of steps inside only faintly visible when full.

On the west wall was our pride and joy, the *shir*. *Shir,* in Persian, has several meanings. One is milk. The other is lion and third is a tap. The object on the wall combined the last two. In fact it was a lion's head carved out of stone with its mouth open. Like a ringed bull, it had a metal ring through the nose, but it wasn't quite a ring, more like a railway alarm chain. One pull and a shower of silvery water cascaded out of the lion's mouth. To pull it, was a sure way of stopping a soap-blinded child from yelling, or a timid one from refusing to enter the bath.

This was the usual routine. First of all, we wrapped a red cotton cloth (called a *longe*) round our waists, for the sake of propriety, and sat on upturned flat metal tubs. Warm water was fetched from the basin and poured over our bodies. After a quarter of an hour we were ready for phase one, the *kiseh*. This was a coarse hair cloth woven in narrow strips and sewn into hand gloves. This was dampened and rubbed over lightly with a cake of dry paste shaped like a small round chocolate. Then your skin would be rubbed with the *kiseh*, starting with the hands, arms, shoulders and ending at your feet. The soles were actually rubbed with a pumice stone. This was most ticklish. As a film of grime and dead cells was rubbed away, the skin underneath glowed pink and tingled pleasantly. Then you were rinsed and the next phase, the hairwashing, began. This was horrid, as a large bar of nasty smelling household soap was used and the hands that used it were often heavy. One was told that if one kept one's eyes closed soap would not get into them, in which case, however, how could one see whether it was true or not? Sometimes my mother would find bars of perfumed European soap like 'Palmolive', which was nice, but stung the eyes none the less. They let you go once your hair squeaked, which was a sign of cleanliness. The last phase was the easiest. Another hand glove called *leaf*, this time made of cotton, was thoroughly soaped and rubbed over your skin until you were totally white and slippery. A quick rinse and now you had the choice of two treats, either the *shir* shower or a dip in the fathomless *khazineh*. They both held their fun and their terror equally for us.

The shower, in theory lukewarm, was in practice not always so. What was called the mixer mechanism often failed. Consequently the lion either vomited hot water, or very cold. You couldn't know which until you pulled it and then it was too late. As we insisted on pulling the chain ourselves we had to put up with the shock. It was fun nevertheless.

The *khazineh* was even more terrifying. Before dipping, the water temperature was lowered by means of a cold tap. The *dalak* (professional body-washer) stood on the first step and holding you by the hand, lowered you into its perilous depths. You moved your legs about without touching a thing and your hair floated on the surface of the water like a dark rag. Then you held your breath, dipped your head quickly and surfaced. But supposing the hands that held yours were not strong enough to support you? Or perhaps she did not like you and let you go, what would happen in that unfathomable wilderness? You were told that you would drown. You would gurgle like a water jar in a pond and then sink to the bottom. I always asked the *dalak*, before dipping, if she liked me and invariably she answered, "When you're good".

Once in the water, I always thought of the substructure of the bath which was the nearest thing to Hell I had ever seen. A door to the west of the bathhouse led into a long, steep flight of stairs, without handrail, which descended into a pit stacked with tons of coal. A series of black passages led to a huge, savage furnace. This was lit twice a week in the evenings and attended to all night by a boilerman. Thus the hot water basin and the flues which ran underneath the tiles were heated. For lack of scientific planning the cold water basin would have been heated too. So it was necessary to fill it on the morning of the bath day. On one occasion the tiles got so hot that cold water had to be splashed on them before anyone could step on them and often for "technical" reasons the bath could not be ready until midday or even the evening. When this happened, we were served with a meal in the bath, which was fun. My cosiest recollection of this concerns braised lambs' trotters and pickled cucumber eaten by candlelight, sitting on an upturned tub with a *longe* wrapped round my waist. Tongues of candlelight danced about the wet, dark room and for a moment changed the *hammam* into a mysterious under-sea cavern. Hence the banquet.

Chapter 27

TO SCHOOL

There is a rhyme about the start of a Persian school week which falls on Saturday. It goes like this:

> *Ay Shanbe Narazi*

meaning:

> Oh! Unhappy Saturday,
> Thou causest our feet to bleed,
> As a result of beating,
> With fresh Morello cherry canes.

My sisters and I were up bright and early, having each acquired a new satchel, stationery and books. We were wrapped in hateful black *chadors*, and started walking to school. A woman servant walked behind us carrying our satchels and occasionally telling us not to skip.

Gol was surprised to see us arrive so early, but she let us in and told us where to leave our things. She also told us where our classroom was and where Maryam was to go. She, alas, would be separated from us, but there was no help for it. We went into the school yard which was paved with large flagstones and tried to warm ourselves in the early morning sun. Soon other children turned up in ones and twos, mostly chaperoned. Then we heard a donkey braying and we peeped out through the other side of the maze and saw a richly caparisoned donkey with two little girls on it and a man walking alongside. Someone told us that they were the daughters of the Poet Laureate riding to school on their white donkey. Suddenly the school seemed full of noise and movement and some girls were playing hopscotch the moment they arrived, even before taking off their *chadors*.

A handbell sounded. The children formed themselves into a line two abreast, but instead of holding hands as they did on the first day, they stood half facing outwards, stretching out their arms, palms down, for the *nazim's* (or supervisor's) inspection. She was the same frowning woman we had seen the first day. Her black hair was drawn well back from her face and tied in a bun. She had a stern face and tight lips. Her name was Banu Khanum (both these words mean "lady", *Banu* being an ancient word and *Khanum* a modern one). Her surname was Behzadi. She was a Zoroastrian. Carrying a whip, she marched up and down the line inspecting hands and occasionally flicking the whip lightly at some dirty nails. She stopped once or twice and inspected some of the girls' hair for lice.

When she had inspected one side of the line she quickly went round to the rear and came up on the other side. An unfortunate girl, who feared she would not pass the inspection, tried to switch places with the girl on her left who had. She was not nimble enough and was discovered. The *nazim* rushed up, pulled her out of the line and gave her an indiscriminate thrashing with the whip. Her neck, arms and hips all came under the blows. During the terrified silence which ensued, the words of the 'Lady Bride' flashed across my mind - "the sour-faced Gabre". So this was it.

Then, as though to relieve the tension, a tall, white-skinned girl came slowly down the stairs carrying a large register and a pencil. The *nazim*, having spent her rage, took the book and began to shout out interminable names, some of them tongue twisters. Every time a name was called, the response was *"hazir"* (present) and sometimes a feeble murmur of "she it not here" or "absent". The *nazim* would then mark the book. The roll call seemed to go on for ages and when it was finally over she rang the handbell. At the sound of this, the girls relaxed and climbed the stairs, walking cheerfully through the gallery to their respective classrooms. We forgot all about the unfortunate sobbing miscreant who was taken by kind Gol into her room where her bruises were washed and dressed.

* * *

On my first day, I was asked to sit on the front bench of the classroom with two other girls. Both appeared to be Moslems as they had white skins and short, curly hair. They were about my size. One was called Parvin and the other Pari, which was strange, as I thought I was the only girl of that name. Pari sat between Parvin and me. Her very first words to me, uttered in a deep baritone voice, were:

"My father is concerned with the League of Nations (*Jamee Melal*). Do you know what it means?"

"It is a compound of two Arabic words meaning . . . " I hesitated, "something or the other."

"Precisely," she agreed. "He is very."

"Very what?"

"Very concerned with the League of Nations. So is my brother. They are both at the Foreign Office. Where is yours?"

"At home."

"I mean, what does he do?"

I told her. The meaning of the two words she had used were not clear to me. Had I known what the Foreign Office meant I would have understood her aptitude for diplomacy. She pointed out three girls to me, two of whom had lost their mothers and one her father, and said, "You must remember not to mention their dead parents as it would be painful for them." Suddenly remembering something, she looked startled.

"Who was the lady who brought you here last Wednesday?"

"My mother."

"Your very own?"

"Yes. Of course."

She heaved a sigh of relief. "Isn't it terrible? One can always make a mistake."

I didn't know what I was supposed to say.

"Two other matters. Never mention eggs to Mehri, whose father sells them, or public baths to the Menshadi girls. It is their means of livelihood."

"I know that bath. We passed it on our way to school. What is the teacher's name?"

"She is called Banu Khanum and she is in charge of this class. There are three Banu Khanums among the staff and we have got the ugliest."

86

I looked at the teacher again. She was indeed ugly. She was short and very fat with purplish-black skin. Her greasy black hair was pulled back like the Superintendent's and, whereas that lady had a firm sergeant major type of figure, her namesake was flabby and fleshy. Her face was covered in pimples. She was probably in her early twenties, but was so dull-eyed and unsmiling that she looked much older.

"What is her family name?"

"Who is whispering?" barked the pimples. "You, new girl, don't you realise you mustn't talk in the classroom?"

I was confused and blushed, but Pari, undeterred, held her notebook to her mouth and continued with a stream of information. It was difficult to know whether to listen to her or to the teacher. My other difficulty was not knowing how to respond to a public snub.

The teacher had a huge register open in front of her on the desk. She made marks in it with ink. The marks were from zero to ten. There were columns for each lesson and one for behaviour. In theory, these were independent of one another, but in fact, if you offended the teacher you got a row of zeros against your behaviour column and all the subject columns.

This information came in a low voice from behind Pari's notebook. It already looked as though the forty-five minutes of lessons was going to be an interminable bore, mainly because the teacher had no original ideas, and partly because she never stopped picking at her pimples.

Chapter 28

THE STARING MATCH

The next time we visited Meshkin-Abad was on a public holiday. Curiously, everything seemed to have changed, not in the normal, seasonal way, but in a fundamental way since we had last been to the village. As we left the city, the mountains on the right-hand side of the road had acquired a new majesty and colour. The bare trees in the valley looked like old friends rediscovered and we found a great joy in the freedom from school.

As we approached Meshkin-Abad, a pack of dogs came out to greet us and, with deafening barks, followed the car for nearly a mile to the gate.

It was beginning to snow and the rooms were bitterly cold. Ahmad-Agha, the gardener, was asked to light a fire. He brought in an armful of camel thorn, stuck it in the fireplace and put a match to it. There was a delicious crackling sound and a bright flame. In half a minute it was burnt out. On the next armful he put a few damp logs but they smoked and gave out no heat.

"This really isn't good enough," my mother complained. "You are supposed to look after this place and get it ready for us when we return."

Ahmad-Agha opened his mouth and blew at the smouldering logs.

"I have a brilliant idea," said my eldest brother, Ali. "With the right machinery these camel thorns could be compressed into briquets and used as firelighters."

"Not in time to keep us from freezing to death," said mother crossly. Then she turned to the man. "Now Ahmad-Agha, how do you heat your own room?"

"I have a small charcoal brazier under my *korsi*."

"Bring the brazier into the next room and we will make a *korsi*."

Papa was about to intervene, but thought better of it.

Immediately everyone got busy. A low, square table called a *korsi*, was dragged out of the stores and put in the middle of the adjoining room on the carpet. A few large quilts, called *lahaf*, were spread over the table so that they overlapped and overhung. Mattresses and cushions were arranged all round the table, a length of embroidered cotton was spread on top for grace and the brazier was put directly underneath the middle of the table. Soon we were all seated on the mattresses with our backs leaning on the cushions and our feet stretched under the quilt and warmed by the gentle heat of the charcoal.

"Poor Ahmad-Agha," ventured my father. "What will he do now that we have taken his away?"

"Light himself another," replied mother. "There are a lot in the storeroom."

Papa had a glass of arak while the rest of us had tangerines. By now, the fire in the outer room was blazing away and a large copper vessel of rice was heating on a tripod over it. Mohammad-Beg, the overseer, had come to give Papa the latest news.

"Yes," he replied, "the fruit trees had been pruned, the cattle-shed has been repaired. A donkey had died of a mysterious disease." The answers, like the questions, seemed unconnected and without detail. "Yes," he confirmed, "we too had plenty of rain, the River Ostour flooded and its south bank was waterlogged. And I expect you heard that Ahmad-Agha's latest baby died last week?"

"No, I hadn't," said Papa evenly. "Where is Zanbouz? I didn't see him among the dogs today. Is he dead?" he asked casually.

"We don't know. He has not been seen for six days. The last time he came for his food was on Saturday. At first, people said he had gone after a bitch to Farokh-Abad, but he would have been back by now."

We caught snippets of this conversation through the open door. When it came to Zanbouz, we pricked up our ears. We prayed that he might not have been eaten by wolves, as the place would never be the same without him. Ironically, we were unmoved by the death of the baby. We didn't even know it had been born. After all, it was common knowledge that, apart from their first daughter who survived, Zainab had a child every year who died either at birth or later. In any case, birth and children were grown-ups' business and had nothing to do with us. Mother, on the other hand, seemed very upset by the news. She called the gardener after supper and gave him money and food as well as some warm clothing which she had brought along for Papa and herself.

The next day, the men went out shooting. My father, Mohammad-Beg and my two eldest brothers had guns and the boys, Jamshid, Ismail and Karim, followed with sticks. Karim was growing up fast, but he looked lost in my father's cast-off Army shirt and hat. He was a fairly good shot and had an uncanny knack of finding game. In those days in Persia, pheasants and partridges were not bred for sport. They were wild and you had to search for them.

The snow, which had ceased during the night, started again by the time they got back with a deer and a bag of birds. Persians never hang their game as in England. Any smell of putrefaction is distasteful to them. In winter, game is buried under the snow in lidded copper vessels to tenderise them. Deer meat is marinated in onion and barbecued immediately.

On that day, Soghra came to bake bread. We were determined to show off our new knowledge to her.

"How long did you bake today?" we asked.

"I started after breakfast and baked till noon," was the simple answer.

"How many loaves did you make?" we persisted.

"You see that wooden vat?" she said good-naturedly, pointing to a huge, wooden vessel like a half-barrel. "I baked all the dough inside it."

"How much does my mother pay you?"

"She gives me sugar, tea and clothes for my little boy. Medicine, of course."

Really! It suddenly seemed so unnecessary to learn arithmetic.

"I believe you all go to school now. Do you like it?" she asked wistfully.

"No. Hate it."

At that moment, there was a disturbance at the gate of the outer garden. Three labourers stood there with a dead jackal at

90

their feet, the side of its head bashed in. A yellow, filthy and emaciated beast was sniffing at the blood which trickled down its jaw. It was Zanbouz.

"What has happened?" we asked in great excitement. "Where did you find him?"

The men only spoke Turkish. Ahmad-Agha, who was following them, translated:

"These men were working on the far side of the Ostour River, digging a channel for the flood water, when they heard barking from inside a dry well. They approached and looked down. There were Zanbouz and the jackal sitting at the bottom of the well staring at each other. They must have been down the well for the last six days at least. One of the men was lowered into the well. He knocked the jackal on the head with his spade and brought the dog out."

We were overjoyed to see our old friend and favourite escort, and tried to clean him up. He ate a whole loaf ravenously and practically drank dry the little stream which runs through the garden. His luck was in, for most of the barbecued meat was so tough that it was only fit for a dog.

After this feat of endurance, Zanbouz secured himself a special place in Meshkin-Abad. He was no longer 'untouchable'.

Chapter 29

THE BUFFALOES

The novelty of being thrust into school soon wore off, and we settled for the dull necessity of being educated. It was a boring business, but had a few compensations, such as the daily walk to and from school.

After a hurried breakfast of tea, bread and cheese, and sometimes the tearful refusal of the stale egg we were offered, we made a desperate search for our satchels, right shoe or whatever. We went out through the garden gate into the avenue, turned left towards the North, and came face to face with the massive snow-capped Albourz Mountains, which we invariably greeted with salaams.

"It looks as though we shall be in for a cold winter," volunteered our chaperon. However, we were not interested in the weather.

Our avenue was called Yousef-Abad because it led northwards to the garrison district of that name, which now housed the great National Iranian Oil Company building. During that period, north of the crossroads where Avenue Naderi intersected Avenue Yousef-Abad was all desert, apart from a few large private gardens.

Once in Avenue Yousef-Abad, there were two main routes with several minor diversions that we could take to school. We took the broad route up Yousef-Abad, turned right at the crossroads into Avenue Naderi, turned left at the next major crossroads into *Kuche* Arbab and there on the left was the school.

But, not so fast. We had plenty of time. We were going to see how many houses we knew in the neighbourhood by touching their doors. First, on the east pavement, there was the Rajaboff's house. They were my mother's friends, Russo-Caucasian, most sophisticated and very "Society". Khanum Rajaboff never ceased laughing, and adored us. We crossed the road and boldly touched her door. The next known house was on our side of the road, so we crossed the road again. No problem here at all. There was no traffic whatsoever, except for a few stray dogs in the distance. This gate was in the wall of a large park. It had once in the past belonged to the Regent and was now the property of Aalam-e-Saltaneh. My parents knew them so we surreptitiously brushed our fingers against the gate. Walking on the same side for a few hundred yards we had an argument. Should we touch the door of one or both houses which belonged to the Doctor.

"He doesn't live in them both."

"But he owns them."

Approaching the first door, we saw a large, white plaque inscribed in Latin characters (which we couldn't read) and Persian ones (which we could) "The Italian Club". We decided to leave it alone. Instead we whole-heartedly touched the house which was inhabited by our friend, his wife and family, including his eldest half-blind son and his family.

92

We called the Doctor "Legion" because he wore the insignia of the *Legion d'Honeur*, which had been granted to him by the President of France. His name was Dr. Saghafi. He had been personal physician to a former King, Mozafare-din-Shah, and had accompanied him on his European travels. All in all, he had visited Europe fourteen times, an impressive figure for those days of difficult travel and high costs. Apart from a remarkable beauty of visage and manners, there was an aura of high culture about him. He was constantly writing to learned societies in Europe and publishing books. He was locally known by his title, Aalam-e-Doleh.

Years ago, my sister Gohar's death in his surgery had given him a bad shock. Apart from his personal distress, he had expected reprisals. At the time of the event, my father was Minister of the Interior with wide-reaching powers, and Persians can be pretty merciless when a life has been lost, whatever the cause. The poor doctor had expected to be (at the least) hanged. When time passed and no prosecution came, he was so grateful that he vowed to treat our entire household free of charge as long as he practised - the wags said "at your own risk," - but he was in fact indispensable as a friend and doctor, and my family owed him much.

What with talking, trying to eat pistachio nuts with one hand and holding our *chador* under the chin with the other, our progress was slow. On the other pavement we could see the private garden of Saghat-Dule-Diba, now the Park Hotel. Opposite his gate on our side, a cottage hospital was being built, dedicated to his mother.

We now reached the crossroads, on the corner of which stood the white building of the Armenian Club. Round the corner, we bumped into Taghi and his donkey, heavy under a load of hot, cooked beetroot. He stopped and asked after the family, particularly the "Colonel", meaning Jamshid, who in his early wild days, had organised an army of the local barrow boys and drilled them in the open spaces near our house. He had decorated his soldiers with wooden medals and sashes made of old sheets. The Colonel had ridden this very same donkey which now carried seasonal fruit and vegetables, and in the summer, ice, for this particular lieutenant. Taghi remembered Jamshid with affection and pressed us to eat some of his beetroot. These were huge, yo-yo shaped, deep red and delicious. We politely refused.

If we had turned left here, we could have touched many more doors, but we had to turn right into Avenue Naderi which, although still quite primitive, was beginning to become the most fashionable street in Tehran. Men in European clothes could be seen from time to time and even bare-headed European ladies. Armenian ladies always wore hats with short veils. We saw two of the latter, every morning, looking like queens from a pack of playing cards, with thick make-up, velvet hats half covering their foreheads and stiff veils sticking out from under their hats. They sat absolutely motionless against the glass pane behind the decorated metal grill of the window. One was old and wore a black hat, the other was young and wore red. They were invariably seen first thing in the morning only. They never smiled. On reflection, it must have been difficult for them to keep a straight face, watching three identical Dalek-like creatures skipping about and eating nuts.

Further along the road, a door opened directly onto a flight of stairs leading down into the bowels of the earth. Up the steps came red-faced, clean-looking men, women and children, carrying large bundles. Red and blue *lungis* flew like Union Jacks from the vaulted mud roof to dry in the wind. This was the Menshadi public baths doing a roaring trade, without any competitors in the district. Further along there was a shoe-shop and a pharmacy displaying a foetus in a jar of alcohol, and a gigantic poster showing a collection of fruit and advertising Eno's Fruit Salts. The most remarkable thing about Naderi Avenue was the difference in character between its north and its south side. The south had a distinctive Armenian flavour. The language sounded rich and gutteral, almost like a turkey gobbling, whereas the sound emanating from the north side was woody and consonant-bound, which sounded like a weird game-bird (whistling almost). Ancient names like Goshtasb and Qumarth abounded in the language, as well as Hormoz and Rustam, whose descendants were of greatly diminished stature. Gol's poor consumptive brother was called Rustam.

The narrow lanes running off to the north of Naderi housed what my uncle had called my ancestors - the ancient race of the Zoroastrians. They came from the dry cities bordering the old Dead Sea, now known as the Kavir; places like Kashan, Yazd and Kerman. Everything about them was dry and old, even the children. No glamour, no dash, no joy of living, hardly any living at all. It seemed they were there to represent history like hieroglyphics.

An old man sat in the doorway of his tiny house talking to another old man. He often sat in the sun, presumably to save heating his small living-room, which you could sometimes get a glimpse of. He was toothless and flabby-skinned and had scanty hair and thickish lips. He squatted on the pavement wearing loose blue cotton trousers which covered, but could not hide, his colossal scrotum.

"Why is he like that?" we asked our escort.

"Oh! It's a money bag," was the quickly invented answer. "He keeps his money in his trousers."

***

It was my turn to collect the notebooks today. I took them to the desk, laid them down and stood by, motionless, awaiting further instructions.

The teacher was busy making marks in the register with one hand and picking at her pimples with the other. Fascinated, I looked to see what it was that needed such constant plucking. Suddenly she turned round with lightning speed and gave me a resounding slap in the face. The impact caused me to wobble. This unexpected performance tickled the class and they burst out laughing. It took me a few seconds to take in the nature of this assault. Then tears welled up in my eyes. What had I done wrong? Why the slap and now this ridicule? Should I just stand there and be hooted at? No. I decided to walk to my desk which was in the front row, but the teacher suddenly shouted, "Get out of my sight. Get to the back of the room!"

We usually sat in the classroom according to height, and, I suppose, age. The younger ones in front and the older ones behind. Now, looking back, there must have been a tremendous difference of age between the youngest and the oldest. In those days they did not move you up as you got older, but according to your exam results. If you failed you stayed in the same class and joined the new girls.

Some of the pupils in the back reminded me of buffaloes. They were very old, with large hands and feet and large, pendulous breasts. They had darkish blue skins, dull eyes, greasy black hair drawn back from the face and worn in a single fat plait. I always shrank from them because they had thick lips with a spot of shiny, dry saliva at each corner.

Seeing me approach, the buffaloes squeezed their fat, dark bulks against the wall and made room for me on the bench. I looked desperately about for an alternative, but there was none. I sat gingerly on the edge of the bench while one of them whispered to me very slowly, "Do not cry. Try and forget about it."

Forget about it. My God! I could not even understand why it had happened, let alone forget it. The weight of the injustice began to crush my heart and I sobbed aloud. I felt a large damp hand on my head pressing me gently but firmly towards sweaty breasts. It was strangely comforting. "Here you are," said a drawling voice. "Take my handkerchief and wipe your nose. It is dripping." I obeyed.

"Why did she hit me?" I asked, in between sobs.

"Because you stared at her. She doesn't like it."

After I calmed down I asked, "What is your name?"

"Morvarid (Pearl). My sister's name is Homayun (Royal) and the one sitting in front of us is my cousin, Laal (Ruby)."

Had I been less indifferent to the meaning of the words, or less unhappy, I might have laughed, but there was also something kind, calm and soothing about this trio.

Once my repulsion at their appearance was shed, I became quite friendly with the 'Buffaloes'. During the rest period which followed, they told me about their relatives who seemed to include most of the Zoroastrians in the school. Unlike the Foreign Office girl, they could speak objectively about people. I mentioned the peculiar old man who sat on the pavement and whom we passed on the way to school.

"Old Rustam!" they exclaimed. "He is our mother's cousin."

"Why does he keep his money bag in his trousers?"

They laughed loud and long, slapping their sides. "It is not a money bag. It is a disease."

I was most impressed by their candour. I would never have claimed such a monstrous second cousin.

Chapter 30

THE DISASTER

Granny Bishana's room was a sanctuary. My sisters and I could indulge in various misdeeds whilst in there, without being detected or corrected. In fact it was considered dutiful and noble of us to keep the old lady company. There, we ate stolen sweets, abused one another and generally neglected our homework.

Bishana was hard of hearing and almost blind. We entered her room and greeted her in a very loud voice, "Salaam."

"Salaam-*e-Aleikom* my child. Which one are you?"

We identified ourselves.

"Come and sit down and tell me all your news."

"No news."

"So what have you been doing all day?"

"This is early morning."

"Is it indeed? Such a long morning!"

At this point someone else would enter who might have some news. "They are changing the water in the pond," or "I am going out this afternoon to buy shoes." Usually something neutral which would not distress her, unlike a death or a servant leaving.

After picking our brains she would come out with her own interesting and lucid account of events - always in the past. When she was describing something, she did not sound deaf but had a clear voice and beautiful diction. She had a formal mode of speech and almost a Saadian turn of prose.

"Gol Pari," she would say out of the blue, meaning me and pointing to my sister Maryam. "You are my mother-in-law."

A quick calculation would reveal that I would have been 130 years old.

After a long pause during which one assumed that she had lost the thread of her thoughts, she would resume, "Your namesake and great-grandmother was a valiant woman. She rode like the wind and fought like a warrior." Another long silence - suddenly,

"Is it true that you are afraid of horses?" There was no scorn, just speculation. I groped for an answer.

"Only when they bray."

"You mean neigh," corrected Zari.

"What was that?" Granny would inquire.

"She is afraid, Bishana. She is a coward," came the child's verdict. Another long pause.

"Your great grandfather, Pasha Khan, had a curious destiny. He considered himself lucky to have come after the upheavals of the Thirty Years War, which had uprooted his ancestors so many times. He possessed some land in the country and lived with his wife and five children in Tabriz.

"One night he was awakened with a terrible jolt and before he realised what was happening the ceiling collapsed, burying his wife and three children. By the time he had groped in the dark and dragged the other two children out into the safety of the garden, the rest of the house had collapsed. He had experienced earthquakes before, but nothing like this. He rushed about trying to get help, but found no houses standing and only a handful of shocked survivors moaning and calling for help. Stunned and bereaved, Pasha Khan and the children made their way to the suburbs of the city where his widowed sister lived. To his amazement, he found her unharmed and with a roof over her head. After explaining the situation, he left the children there and went back to see if there was any chance of digging the rest of his family out or, at best, their corpses.

"By now, dawn had broken and the sight which met his eyes filled him with despair. There was complete destruction. Half of the local mosque had vanished, the public bath was a heap of rubble and there was nothing left of the thriving bazaars. There was a weird silence. As he neared his old home he saw flames shooting out of the ruins of his house. There was no hope. That was the great Tabriz earthquake that killed thousands of people. There was no question of outside aid. Each had to fend for himself.

"As he had lost his home and all his possessions he had to take immediate steps to keep the surviving children alive. His sister agreed to look after them while he went to his farm in Ardebil to raise money and get provisions. It took him three weeks to get to the farm, sell a field and bring back money and a modest store of food. He arrived back late one evening and banged on the door of his sister's house. There was no reply. Thinking they were asleep, he shouted and banged louder, but still nobody replied. Eventually he broke in and found the house empty.

"The city was still in utter desolation and he could not think of a soul to whom he could turn for help. Frantically he searched for someone who could tell him where his sister and his children had gone to. He found an old hag who told him they had been carried off by the cholera which had swept through the city.

"'Where are they buried, and who officiated?'

"'Who officiated?' laughed the old woman. 'God help you innocents! Don't you know that half the survivors of the earthquake died from cholera and the grave-diggers had to be buried themselves? In the end soldiers had to be called in from Marand to dig mass graves. Where have you been all this time? This city has seen earthquake, fire and cholera and the population has been reduced to a handful of old and ugly ones like me who were spared because we frightened Izrail.'

"Pasha Khan did not wait for her hooting laughter to cease. He ran out, a shattered man. In two strokes his whole past had been obliterated. He walked back to his sister's house and went through the rooms looking for a memento of his lost family, a child's shoe or a toy, something which had belonged to his sister; but all had been cleared. There was nothing to suggest that his family had ever lived. What a terrible mistake to have left his children behind. But then they might have died on the way.

"The empty rooms seemed to devour him. The walls seemed to hem him in, as in a grave, or hurl him from side to side. In panic he grabbed his sheepskin *pusteen* and fled.

"There was a *saku* or stone seat in the corner of the ruined *maidan*. He sat on it that night and it became his home for the next two years. He sat there, day in, day out. Life gradually returned to normal and people who had fled the pestilence came back. Children appeared and began to tease him. Kind women brought him food. Birds and insects settled on him and cats and dogs shared the shelter of his *pusteen* at night. Like some famous Franki holy man, he communicated with animals and birds and they were not afraid of him. His hair and beard grew long, and although he was only in his late thirties, he looked like an old man.

"One or two acquaintances who had escaped the calamity came and spoke to him. They said it was not dignified for a man to behave in this manner and that he must rise above his misfortunes. He mildly asked them 'Where to and why?'

"There is no doubt that he would have died of self-neglect had not Gol Pari Khanum, a young and brave woman, taken charge of him. She did not know fear and it is possible that she put him to shame by the example of her own courage and spirit. She married him and took him to her property near lake Urumieh. This, like most settlements of those days, was a stockaded house attached to a farm. Here Pasha Khan regained his balance and a degree of serenity.

"One winter's day when the world was covered in snow and he had gone to the nearby village, Gol Pari Khanum heard a persistent knocking on the outside wall of the cattle shed. She climbed onto the flat roof and looked down. A couple of robbers were digging a hole in the wall with an axe. Unruffled, she looked around for a weapon. Her eyes fell upon a heavy, stone garden-roller used in the summer to reinforce the mud and straw roofs of Persian houses. She quietly rolled this to the edge of the wall, immediately above the men's heads, and waited until they stepped back to survey their work. Then she gave the roller a quick push. It fell with a great thud, knocking out one of the thieves. The other ran away. She came down and tied the man up. It was all over by the time her husband came back.

"They had two sons, Safar-Ali-Khan, a brave and compassionate soldier who, alas, never married. The other was my second husband and your grandfather, Mohebali-Agh."

And under her breath, she added in Turkish, "The simpleton."

Chapter 31

ROZE

My sisters and I were now considered old enough to attend a *Roze*. This was a very interesting experience and I feel inadequate in trying to describe it. My dictionary defines *Roze* as "description of the tragedy of Karbela", when various Imams - descendants of Prophet Mohammad - were murdered by their political rivals. The nearest European equivalent would be a shortened version of Bach's St. Matthew Passion, in which one singer takes the part of all the solo singers and the audience acts the part of the choir - this attached to a straightforward Sunday sermon, with a bit of elementary Sunday School teaching thrown in.

I do not know whether *Roze* is peculiar to the Shia sect only, but I cannot see what use the Sunis could have for this sort of passion, as they suffered no martyrdom. It is quite possible that *Roze*, like *Taazia* (a Shia Passion play), was originally introduced at the time of the Safavids when Shiism and Persian nationalism had their revival and were officially encouraged.

Anyway, *Roze* has several aspects. One is the need of the devout to feed their souls with the story of the tragedies, thereby bringing themselves nearer to their beloved saints. I had an old aunt who, as long as I could remember, had engaged a clergyman to come to her house every Friday eve to sing a *Roze*. On the arrival of the man, two chairs would be brought into the otherwise bare room. The mullah, after taking off his shoes, would sit on one chair while the other one would be left vacant. My aunt would come in, wrapped in a *chador*, and crouch on the floor. As the mullah sang, she wept silently for approximately ten minutes, then got up and went into the pantry where she washed up the tea-things while the mullah sang to the empty chair. At the end of half-an-hour, the old man would stop and cough discreetly, at which signal Madame would appear and give him some money before he left. In her case, I really think it was a genuine, but moderate devotion to the saints, as well as a desire to help the old mullah. No doubt, many devout individuals as well as trade associations arranged such performances on a large scale, to benefit their fellow beings. But in the case of wealthy citizens, the rich newcomers to society, and those with an axe to grind, it certainly degenerated into a publicity stunt, or even an election campaign.

Mother's friend and neighbour, a dedicated agnostic, if not heretic, had such a performance annually arranged during the month of Moharam. Mother had left earlier by special invitation, and my sisters and I were taken there later by a maid. All draped in black, we entered through the garden gate and immediately saw an extraordinary sight. The whole surface of the large garden was covered with carpets on which black-draped women sat cross-legged in groups. It looked like some macabre zoological island, not that I knew of such a place then.

As we passed each group, I tried to sit down every time I saw another child, or a pretty face, but the maid tugged at my hand, and we went on. Each group seemed to get fatter and less pretty until we got to the very far end of the garden. Here, no one seemed to be under forty and the prettiest face was my mother's. We sat down, refused a glass of tea offered on a silver tray, and began shamelessly staring at all the faces.

Soon there was a commotion and the women hurriedly covered their visages by pulling down their veils. An *akhund*, a middle-aged man in an *aba* and black turban, appeared. He sat on a chair and said a prayer in Arabic which, without a break trailed into highly pedantic Persian. He gave an exposé of life on this earth for a good Moslem, his duties and social obligations; he exhorted his audience to chastity and honesty, and warned them against smug self-deception. He said among other things, that Polé Sarat, the bridge which leads the righteous to the gate of Heaven, is narrower than a hair of your head and longer than eternity. One wrong step and the bridge gives way, you fall into an abyss of darkness where all kinds of terror await you. Everything that you touch is sharper than the point of a needle and more poisonous than a viper's sting. You roll deeper into filth and misery until you are devoured by the leaping flames.

102

He was speaking in a normal, educated voice, but with each sentence the atmosphere grew more tense and charged. Suddenly, judging that the mood was right, he quickly modulated his voice into a sing-song alto and burst into lamentation for the death of Imam Hossain, and the other Imams. How on the eve of the massacre, each said farewell to his mother and sister, and what the women replied (here the voice became very sweet and almost feminine), and how they all suffered; how the men were "feasted" by the accursed Yazid, who fed them on salt and dogs flesh; how the next day, they were subjected to torture and thirst in the desert of Karbela, quoting their last words, and finally, their martyrdom.

At each phase of the lament, women heaved and sobbed and cried out. They poured out their compassion into their black laps. Some beat their breasts and others fainted. By now they had reached such a pitch of emotion that many forgot to keep their faces covered and if the mullah had wished, he could have feasted his eyes. Then, judging that the audience had had enough, he, suddenly and dramatically, dropped his voice to its original low pitch, said a hasty prayer, advised the women to use patience and self-control; then left his seat and with quick steps made for the door, where he was handsomely rewarded by the son of the family.

At the drop of the *akhund's* voice, there was a dramatic transformation. All hysteria ceased, eyes were dried and the last nose blown, and within half a minute the women were chatting amicably among themselves and drinking tea until the appearance of the next performer. Sometimes there were five or six *akhunds* at the same session. *Akhunds* were particularly prized for their clear voice and the ability to project it; also for their power to draw tears from women. A shrewd performer could ask - and was often paid - his own price.

That night I had a nightmare. I suddenly woke up with a terrible sensation of falling, and remembering the *akhund's* words about the flimsy bridge to heaven and the horrors beneath, I opened my eyes to find complete darkness. I screamed in terror. Azra, who slept in the same room, woke up in alarm and asked me what the matter was. I said that I was afraid of going to Hell. She replied that I had a long way to go before I reached it. I could not be con-

103

soled and wanted a light. She said that a light would alarm everyone, and assured me that, according to our Faith, children are
born innocent until they grow up, so that even if I died, I would
not go to Hell immediately. I asked how much longer one had to
wait. She said, "Ages and ages."

"What? Two months, six months, a year?"

"No. Thousands and thousands of years."

"What happens then?"

"Oh! Go to sleep."

"Please, what happens?"

"First, people become bad, mad and stupid. Then comes Dajal
(the anti-Christ); he will come riding on his monstrous ass who can
play a thousand tunes. At each tune a thousand people rush out of
their houses, fascinated. Men and women are indistinguishable, all
dressed and made up in a most exaggerated manner. These follow
the imposter, and the streets become thronged with the wicked.
They are hungry, and although there is plenty of food, they cannot eat."

"Why not? Have they no money?"

"Yes. But money is no longer the currency. It is enough to
say a short prayer *(salavat)* in exchange for goods, but the people
have forgotten how to pray. After the wicked ones have been
lured away to perdition, the Twelfth Imam, whose name must not
be mentioned lightly, will appear. The dead will be resurrected and
everyone judged, rewarded or punished according to their merit."

"But you were talking about the living a moment ago," I protested.

"What is the difference?" she yawned. "What is the difference?"

I have rarely thought about that conversation until just recently, when I found myself in the middle of the King's Road,
Chelsea, one Saturday afternoon. Something that I saw there
reminded me of Azra's words on that dark fearsome night.

Chapter 32

THE LUCKY ONE

I never saw my maternal grandfather, the *Sardar*, and only know three minor facts about him. He was for some years Governor of Esterabad, now Gorgan; he had been due to be hanged during the constitutional crisis in 1908 as he had supported the Shah's despotic rule, and lastly, he had very little imagination. He gave only three names, Abbas, Hossain and Reza to his four sons to share, with variations.

According to all the pictures and family mythology, he had been extremely handsome and aristocratic, and to Mama, his only daughter, he rated one rung above God. His house was like a garrison, teeming with *Nayebs* and Sergeants, who drew their pay from their regiments and their food from his kitchen. In return (again judging from the photographs) they were armed to the teeth, which made him feel good.

Naturally, all his sons were soldiers, except the third boy, who had suffered from poliomyelitis and was disabled. Everyone loved him, but few helped him. He married a sweet girl and had a large family.

The first son, Abbas Gholi, the *Salar*, was straightlaced, a conformist and staid. He was a disappointed man, for he had no sons. It was surprising that he had any offspring at all. He had married a tiny cousin when she was nine years old. She never grew, but was to produce two fairly tall girls.

The second son, Gholam-Reza, was the obvious heir. He had inherited his father's good looks, his style and Olympian outlook. He was a sportsman and an authority on wine.

The third boy, Hossain-Gholi, a poliomyelitis sufferer, was considered unfortunate not being able to be a soldier. No one stopped to think what was so good about being a soldier.

The youngest boy, Reza-Gholi, was the apple of his father's eye. He had good looks and a sardonic sense of humour. He was

sent to be educated, at great expense, to Moscow and St. Peters-
burg. He returned with a little Russian and a lot of syphillis. One
of the *Nayebs* was drafted to look after the young man and to
have him treated with traditional remedies. Unfortunately this
particular *Nayeb* was addicted to opium and believed this to be
the best remedy. So, not only was he not cured of his syphillis,
Reza Gholi became an opium addict as well. Meanwhile he was
commissioned in the Gendarmerie, the first modern Persian police
force. While his family were waiting for him to recover and marry
properly, he was found a *sighé*, or temporary wife, one of the
young village girls. Every time there was talk of arranging a marriage, the girl would have a phantom pregnancy and negotiations
would halt. Long after the *Sardar's* death and the dissolution of
the family home, they were formally married and she produced a
son, who was called Masoud, 'the lucky one'.

The whole family was delighted with this event, but unfortunately it was later discovered that the child's tongue was slightly
deformed.

Long before this unfortunate discovery, when he was only an
infant his parents brought him to Meshkin-Abad for a few days
visit. They also brought a dumpy young nanny. On the first night
the child cried all the time and kept everyone awake. On the second
evening he was well-behaved. In fact so much so, that he did not
want his supper. When my mother heard of this she got worried
and picking him up she found that he was completely limp. Suspic-
ion fell on the nanny, who admitted that she had put a minute
particle of the master's *foor*, or "smoke", in the baby's food. This
got round very quickly and it was decided that his parents should
take him immediately to Tehran to a doctor.

The old Ford was taken out of the vast garage - which also
housed sacks of wheat and a company of mice. Petrol was poured
in from a large tin can, water topped up and belongings and drinking water piled on the floor of the car. Anxious farewells were said
and good wishes exchanged. Then there was a hitch. The petrol
tank of the ancient Ford was in the front. After it had been filled,
Abbas, the chauffeur, looked for the cap, but could not find it.
Everyone else looked with hurricane lamps, candles, torches. It
might have fallen on the gravel, so everyone stooped and touched

106

the ground hoping not to find a snake. On the other hand, it might have been hidden under the luggage, so that was hauled out. A lot of blame and some abuse was hurled around as the situation became desperate. Someone suggested sealing the tank with gauze and plaster, as done to food. Abbas did not think much of it. Meanwhile the baby, warmly wrapped, was held in his nanny's arms.

Away from the circle of light the stars shone brightly and it was a cold, clear night. No one thought of going to bed or sending the children to bed while this drama was being enacted. We must have been standing around the car for over an hour, every moment that passed probably reduced the chance of saving the child. Men were talking of alternative transport to Karaj, such as horses. Had they been able to see into the future they would have let the infant die peacefully that night. Suddenly out of the blue a child yelled. It was Masoud. The cold, fresh air had revived him. The sound fell like sweet music on the ears of everyone present and the parents wept for joy.

Next morning the petrol-tank cap was found on the canvas roof of the car.

Chapter 33

THE WINGED BULL

Our school was founded by Arbab Kaykhosro Shahrukh, a liberal Zoroastrian gentleman with far-reaching ambitions for the education and emancipation of women. He represented the Zoroastrian minority in Parliament, had a number of commercial enterprises and had strong ties with the Parsees of India and many friends in Britain. Our little elementary school was the first step towards realising his ambition. He recognised that if he were to succeed, he had to do things gradually and cautiously. He must first gain the confidence of the parents, the majority of whom were Moslems and therefore narrow-minded.

The next important step was to acquire the support of the Government. In this, he was very fortunate. The timing was absolutely perfect. It was now official policy to rouse nationalism in Persians and spur the population into action through pride in their history. Who better suited to carry this task through than the Zoroastrians, the heirs of our glorious ancestors?

The third step - a negative one - was to avoid any clash with the clergy who were still very influential and could be politically damaging. So our chastity was jealously guarded, any frivolity banned and the teaching of Islamic principles strictly observed.

The standard of teaching was extremely low, simply because there were no educated women in the country at this time, and the men were not allowed in the school, except two very old and decrepit ones. Any woman who could read, write and add could get a job as a teacher at a girls' school. Such women were generally poor, or plain, or both, and not eligible for marriage.

The classes were small but uneven in age. One teacher was in charge of a particular class, teaching grammar, spelling and writing. Other teachers came and taught arithmetic, geography, religion and history. None of these women seemed to have any vocation or understanding of their subject, with the result that most lessons were painfully dull.

Another constricting factor was the geography of the school itself, a seven-roomed building inside an L-shaped brick-paved yard, which contained six classrooms and an office.

The ground on the north side had been levelled to form a platform two or three feet above the rest of the yard. On this platform a lot of hopscotch was played. Nearby, in the north-west corner, there were eight lavatories. Waterless and paperless, these were just holes in the ground with flimsy partitions and doors which opened outwards with only a grip handle on each side, but no bolt or catch.

During the first year when we went home to lunch, we tried to avoid using these loos, as they were incredibly dirty and disgusting. Gol's sickly husband, Ardeshire, was supposed to clear them and fill the tanks with water for ablution, but naturally he found this task distasteful and forgot about it. Later, however, when an annexe was bought on the north-east corner for extra classes, the basement of it was thrown open as a dining-room. From then on parents found it easier to send lunch to school at midday instead of ferrying the children backwards and forwards. This was a bad development as far as our pleasure and "convenience" was concerned, as an eight hour confinement obliged us to use the horrible 'loos'. You took a long breath, ten feet away, ran in and out without taking another breath, your face red and the veins on your neck sticking out. At a safe distance you let out the stale breath.

There was a small aggressive teacher who had two, prominent buck-teeth. She went into the lavatory one day with teeth and came out without. It was rumoured that, for the sake of privacy she used to tie a piece of string to the grip-handle of the door and hook the other end to her front teeth while she crouched on the loo. Suddenly a child had pulled the door, dislodging the string and the teeth.

I avoided the northern zone at all times.

The southern zone on the other hand was quite fascinating. It was bounded by a five-foot high wavy wall, overhung by dark cypresses and pines. The trees belonged to the garden of the Zoroastrian temple called Maabad. This was a square one-story stone building. A cross between a fire temple and a Christian Science Hall. In front it had huge pillars, no windows and two grey stone winged bulls guarding its sacred threshold.

What was so impressive about the place was the absolute peace and serenity of the garden surrounding the temple. There were no blossoming trees and laughing flowers. The garden had been planted with evergreens, dark shrubs and fragrant herbs. The water in the pool was always clean and the paths and gravel were carefully tended by a quiet-moving, almost unseen gardener. Apart from him, the only other visitors were song birds and a fat, dignified old *Mobed*, or Chief Priest, going in at regular hours.

Moslem girls said that he went in to tend to the sacred fire and keep it burning. That was only gossip. No one really knew what he did in the temple. We would have liked to know, but the Zoroastrian girls were not allowed to tell us. In fact, they guarded the secret of their religious rituals most jealously from us. Even the "buffaloes" would not speak. I think they had instructions not to discuss religion. How I wished I could have been admitted to this romantic sanctuary and initiated into its rites, but that was out of the question. The only time we got close to the temple was when we had to traverse its garden on our way to the huge exercise yard which was, in fact, only a *kharabe*, accessible only through the temple garden. On these occasions we were led in a line, walking on tiptoe. The *Nazim* herself led us, and if we looked too closely at the locked doors we were told to respect God's House and to lower our eyes. In the exercise yard, where we ran races and played handball, there were several large, stone slabs. Moslem girls refused to sit on them saying that these were used for laying Zoroastrian corpses on. The birds came later and plucked the eyeballs out. Whether a man was destined for Heaven or Hell was determined by the loss of the right or the left eye. Others claimed that the stone slabs were destined for building material for the construction of a great new school to be built soon. However, we had no way of verifying these rumours.

Close by, there was an institution of an entirely different character. At the end of the wavy wall there was a short flight of steps terminating at the top in a padlocked door. We always assumed that it was part of the offices of the temple. One day, I found the door ajar and looked in from behind velvet curtains. I saw a large hall in complete darkness, but the stage was lit and on it were, what looked like fairies - girls in ballet dresses - dancing to most delicious music which came from nowhere. I stood there spellbound. I had never heard or seen anything so magical before. I must have been there for a long time for the other girls had joined me behind the curtain, enraptured. Suddenly they began to run and I followed them, at the *Nazim's* approach. She flicked her whip at us and padlocked the door. We scattered. I learnt later that this hall was called the "Opera", where singing and ballet were performed every night, starring the great Tamara, but I was never to see inside the place again.

As all the interesting avenues of exploration had been blocked to me, there was nothing for it but to make the best of the least boring lessons. I soon found, that with the best will in the world, it was impossible to make Persian history dull. It had so much drama and colour. Modern books were not available then. Our

110

very first history book did not describe the great deeds of Cyrus and Darius. It was a rendering of the epic poet Ferdosi's *Book of Kings* in prose form.

Ferdosi, the millennium of whose birth was soon to be celebrated, was at that moment the darling of the Zoroastrians and of the authorities.

When the Arabs conquered Persia in the seventh century A.D., they were not only concerned with the destruction of the existing religion but also of the Persian language. There is a story that one hundred years after the conquest, the Arab Governor of Khorasan announced a literary competition. The subject was to write an essay without using a single Arabic word. A few people entered, and the winner of the competition, a young man from noble Persian stock, hoping to take the prize, presented himself to the Governor and had his head cut off - to the discouragement of the others.

Two and a half centuries later, Ferdosi completed his great epic poem, the *Shah-name*, in pure Persian. As he put it himself:

"From poems I shall build such a high citadel
That can never be harmed by wind or rain."

Basing his work on an earlier text, he wrote sixty-thousand verses, weaving together the ancient legends about the lives and deeds of Persian Kings. Of how, one by one, the monarchs taught the Persian people certain skills: ironmongery, animal domestication and writing; how Jamshid the Great founded the Persian calendar on the Vernal equinox, and instituted the Festival of *Noruz*; how he discovered wine-making and taught medicine and the art of government. Being over-clever, however, he eventually forgot his duty to God and claimed deity.

There were monsters, like Zahak, who was cursed with two serpents on his shoulder-blades, which could only be pacified with a daily diet of human brains. And there was Rustam, the great Persian Achilles, whose deeds and bravery inspired generations of Persian boys.

For all his troubles, Ferdosi was not actually beheaded, but he was badly swindled. He had been promised a gold coin for each

111

distich; instead he received silver. The news came to him while he was in a public bath. In anger he distributed the money among the bath attendants and fled the realm.

The religion of the ancient Persians was based on two Gods: Ahura Mazda, God of good, who demanded truth, hard work and sport, and Ahriman, the Demon, who thrived in darkness and on lies. These two were always struggling for supremacy and their success depended on people's support.

I once asked a Zoroastrian whether this belief was still held after the rape of Persia by the Arabs, and the ultimate success of Ahriman. He said that this was a continuous process like the ebb and flow of the tide and that there was no ultimate victory.

As we moved away from ancient times, history did not lose any of its romance. Persians were forced to accept the existence of a monolithic, Arab God, but they satisfied their duality by supporting the House of Bani-Hashem and thus adhering to Shi'ism from an early stage in the history of Islam. They adored Ali, the righteous, the brave, the truthful, a reflection of Ahura-Mazda, who had fought *with* and been wronged by *Moavieh,* the intriguer, the cowardly, the *Ahriman.*

And wasn't it odd that Persia was intermittently at war with Rome and then with Byzantium until its disappearance?

Any period of prosperity was punctuated by devastating wars, in which minarets were made of human heads, entire populations of cities were blinded and other incredible atrocities were committed.

The most humiliating of these invasions happened in modern times, when the glorious reign of the Safavi dynasty was brought to a close by the audacity of a horde of Afghans. They put siege to the great city of Isphahan. The last Safavid, Shah Sultan Hossain, was taken to the high terrace of his palace of Ali-Ghapu, shown the enemy camp-fires and asked what measure should be taken to save the realm. Being a poet, he responded by reciting:

"Come, let us take our pleasures tonight,
  Let us think of the morrow when it is tomorrow."

Tomorrow was a black day. He was forced to capitulate, live in captivity for the next seven years, and finally murdered.

It is said that at the time, Persian morale was so low that a single Afghan could take a group of Persian prisoners, and ask them to wait while he went in search for a knife to cut their throats. And they just waited.

Thank God for modern times!

Chapter 34

DERVISH

He had a long name which I have now forgotten. We knew him as Bishana's Dervish. His regular visits on the last Wednesday of each month, translated into modern economic terms, were no more than begging missions, if we were to reduce actions and situations to their lowest denominator.

His visits in fact were much more beneficial to us than to himself. We prepared ourselves for him and looked forward to seeing him. On the rare occasion that he did not turn up, Bishana became distressed and sent a boy to the Southern districts of Tehran to find if he was all right. The messenger would come back empty-handed; he had not been able to find him. The Dervish saw to that. He was always vague about his place of residence.

He was thin and moved about with a rare grace. He had long sensitive hands and his finger-nails were tinted with henna. Before he sat down on the stone seat by our door, he carefully folded his gown around him. This was a woollen material of a sombre shade. It was fastened at the waist with a cummerbund, a length of folded silk, faded but enchanting in colour. He wore a loose shirt which showed slightly at the neck. His sandalled feet were immaculately clean and his toe-nails were dyed with henna.

After saying a prayer for his benefactress, the great *Khanum*, who was deaf and immobile and whom he had never set eyes upon, he began his recital of *Mathnavi*. This is the highest form of aesthetic thought and visionary experience written by Molavi, the great Sufi poet. The meaning of the words were far above our little heads but the manner of the recital was so accomplished and the voice so perfect that we stood there spellbound. There was none of the *akhund's* trick of playing with one's emotions. He was not aware he had an audience. It sometimes seemed to me that, like a bird, he was spiritually flying near the clouds, impersonal and almost disembodied.

With childish liberty, we stared at him while he sang. He wore a tall Dervish's hat, had a beard and gentle, hazel eyes. It was impossible to determine his age - young or old, or both. He seemed so pure, so grave. Our eyes invariably rested on his begging bowl or *kashkul*, a boat-shaped bowl made of pewter and covered in engravings and symbols. This was slung on his shoulder by a chain.

After the recital was over, a servant would take his bowl to the kitchen, fill it with food that had been specially prepared for him, and bring it to him together with one *Abasi* (now discarded unit of money equal to one old penny) the gift of the *Khanum*. The Dervish would carefully rearrange the food inside the bowl, cover it with a piece of flat bread, sling the *kashkul* on his shoulder, stick the money in the fold of his gown, say another prayer and depart. The servants had at last understood how fastidious he was about food. Once they had given him messy food and although he had not complained at the time, he had looked disgusted and this had put them to shame.

He never called more than once a month and he never asked for money. When it was given to him he accepted it, gratefully, without effusion. We often wondered how he lived.

Chapter 35

LOSSES

On our third summer holiday from school, we lost a prophet and
two dogs.

Our elder brothers were now well-established in their respective posts. The eldest, Safar-Ali, a mathematician and chemist, was
living in a mountain fastness with a handful of foreign advisers,
where he was building a munition factory. The second, Nosrat, tall,
thin and keen on music was working in the Army Supply Depart-
ment. And the third boy, Mohammad-Vali, the most energetic of
all three, was attached to the Army Engineering Corps. The last
two lived at home in the guest's villa and joined us for meals. They
had no summer holidays as such, but sometimes turned up at
Meshkin-Abad unexpectedly at the weekend.

One night in early July, dogs were barking persistently and
two shots disturbed the peace of the village. In the morning, we
learnt that our brother Vali had telephoned the garrison in Karaj
asking them to send a message to the village asking for the car to
be sent out for him to Karaj the next day. The message was delivered by a soldier on horseback. The messenger had been attacked
by the dogs and he had fired shots in defence, one of which had
hit Fandogh in the stomach. Mohammed-Beg, the overseer, was in
deep distress. He had loved and tended the fiercest dog in the
village and was now about to lose him. We went to his room where
Fandogh lay, his belly crudely sewn up by Mohammed-Beg himself
with a large needle. Although he was still breathing, he was limp
and motionless. We were all touched as the man wept openly, saying that the dog had been his father.

Papa was very angry. He went to Karaj that morning and protested to the young garrison commander about the unnecessarily
cruel act. The soldier was found and questioned. He admitted
shooting "the black and white devil", but pleaded self-defence. He
said that the dog had been climbing up the horse's tail and would

have torn him apart, had he not fired.

And so died the lion of Meshkin-Abad.

***

We had not seen the shepherd Karim since the beginning of the holidays. There was a weird rumour going around that he had become a "prophet". He had chosen the entrance of a shallow pothole at the boundary of the village. He refused to see anyone and would only take the food that his mother brought to him each night, although he was never actually seen doing this. And though he had left without taking any matches, it was said a light shone from his residence at night and this somehow gave credence to his holiness.

It was odd, my father reflected, that such a gay, sporting lad should have suddenly had this strange calling, but he did not like to interfere in other people's affairs so long as they remained harmless.

Among our visitors that summer was Haydar, our marvellous ex-gardener. He was the man who would put his hand to anything so long as it had to do with the soil. Years ago, visiting a grandee's garden for cuttings, he had watched the gardener plant daisies and marigolds in the form of Latin characters saying "Bonjour". He came back determined to do the same. He achieved this successfully except that his "B" grew back to front. Later, when we reduced our staff, he leased a large garden in the suburbs of Tehran and grew the best fruit and vegetables in the city. Although illiterate, he was born wise and his advice was always sought. And thus it came about, that my father came to talk to him about Karim, saying:

"I don't know what has happened to the boy. He doesn't seem to have the making of a prophet, still you never know . . ."

"I heard a peculiar story some years ago," said Haydar. "It was brought to the notice of a village elder that a man calling himself a prophet was gathering quite a following. The elder told his informant 'Go and look at this man's mouth and find out if he has any teeth.' The informant came back and reported that the man had a perfect set of teeth. 'In that case,' said the elder, 'he is

116

no prophet and you must expect to be eaten out of house and home.' Now in the case of this boy, we must find out what it is that he wants. Perhaps he is in love."

"That is no problem where Karim is concerned. Such a good-looking chap could marry any girl he wished."

"Well then, perhaps he has been frightened. Have you had any unusual visitors lately?"

"Only Moti-e-Sultan, the former owner of Meshkin-Abad. He was seen sitting by the *ghanet* smoking his pipe (opium) and weeping. That was his second visit."

"Anyone else?"

"Yes," said Papa slowly after a pregnant pause. "A recruiting officer has been reported in the neighbourhood taking names of future conscripts. Damned liberty!" he swore.

Two days later, Papa took his gun and walked to the edge of Karim's hole. And in a very loud voice, he said, "Come out Karim. I'm going shooting. How can I find game without you?"

A tousled head peeped out and seeing that his master was alone, the rest of Karim emerged, looking dusty but otherwise unchanged.

"And hand me that battery torch," said Papa casually. "I need it more than you." Karim crawled down and brought out the torch. They shot for half a morning as though nothing had happened, before Papa stopped at the gate of the *ghaleh* and asked Karim to go home.

***

The third incident that happened during the summer holiday was quite heart-breaking, as far as we were concerned.

Jamshid, following the advice of our neighbour, Amir Monazam, was experimenting with eggs. He tried to get a hen to hatch guinea-fowl eggs. That failed. Next he got a hen to hatch duck eggs. Three were hatched; two were taken by predators and only one survived. It became velvety, yellow and round. Everyday we watched, amused, as the duckling floated on the little brook that passed through the garden and the anxious mother hopped, from side to side, trying to save it. We called her 'Duck Mother'.

117

At night, the hen and her young slept under a large, inverted garden-basket that had lost its bottom. To secure this, the hole was covered with a large flagstone which was laid on it each evening. Once or twice, a dog called the 'Tiflis puppy' had been shooed away from the basket. This was a peculiar creature, long, yellow and blue-eyed. Its sex was indeterminate. It looked more like a bitch than a dog but behaved like neither. Papa had for some time suspected it of hen-stealing.

One morning, when the basket was lifted, the duck mother was found to be alone and her pretty little duckling gone. What was touching, was the fact that for a long time afterwards the hen used the same basket for sleeping under.

Papa was so disgusted with the dog that he had it shot. There was, as yet, no humane method of putting them down.

We mourned the duckling and the dog.

Chapter 36

ON BEING A PERSIAN

Years ago, living in England, I had to attend cocktail parties quite frequently. Somehow these occasions reminded me of Persian funerals. There you had feigned unfelt grief and here you feigned interest in words you could not hear and jokes you could not understand. To lighten these ordeals, I made up a little game. I would listen to the loudest voice in the group, pick out words at random, and try to see if I could remember any poems containing these words. For instance, a woman would be shouting:

"We did not like Valetta; full of caravans."

Here was a good word.

"O caravan move slowly, the calm of my life is departing.
    This heart that you transport belongs to my beloved."
or: "Jack has bought a new Ford Zephyr."

"Zephyr, shouldst thou pass on the shores of the River Araxes,
Kiss the dust of its desert and freshen thy breath."

It was odd how easily Hafiz lent himself to the motor trade.

I dared not think how my kind host would have reacted had
he been able to read my thoughts. Perhaps like Montesquieu's
Frenchman he would have exclaimed, "What a most extraordinary
thing! How can one be a Persian?" Or he might be liberal-minded
and say, "What is so extraordinary about being a Persian? You are
an individual living in this community like the rest of us."

Personally I would say it would indeed be extraordinary for
a Persian to live among you and be able to ignore the past completely. The differences in our cultures are too numerous and too
deep.

I remember on one occasion, I mentioned to an English
woman about my own age, that my grandmother had possessed an
African slave. She was quite incredulous and asked what century
that was and in what country. The answer is that although we
were both born in the twentieth century, the society I had opened
my eyes to had not fundamentally changed one bit since Usbek's
imaginary letters to his Harem from Paris in 1713. (Montesquieu,
Lettres Persanes).

To begin with, God was not love, He was everything. He was
in the words that one spoke, the earth on which one lived and the
air that one breathed. His word was law. His punishment universally
feared. It was not necessary to preach to a real Moslem or to res-
train him. He had his own built-in self-restraint in the knowledge
of what was allowed and what was not. For instance, if one used
any form of dishonest money, the food bought with it would not
nourish, the clothes would bring on a rash, and the house would
be completely useless as all one's prayers in that house would be
null and void.

I remember once giving a small sum to a needy woman. She
asked me whether the money came from my own allowance. I said
no, I had played cards with my cousins and won. She said in that
case she could not accept the cash as it would be useless to her.
How one wishes that the income tax collector had the same scrup-
les.

Another deeply-embedded convention was the respect paid to the elderly. A man could be forgiven for being a thief, but not for neglecting his parents. Even after their death, one had to pay homage to their memory. On no account should the young be rude to the old.

Eunuchs received a certain amount of deference. These wizened, beardless persons were sometimes seen escorting a heavily veiled, noble lady through the streets.

It was believed that the body's metabolism was based on things 'hot and cold', which had nothing to do with temperature. Food and certain emotions were similarly classified; grief was hot, while shock was cold. Seasonal blood-letting was considered essential for all, including children, except the very weakest. If an ill person sweated, it meant that he or she would recover. Warts were "persuaded" to dry off by touching them lightly with a single grain of barley, which was then inserted into a sheep's entrails and buried. Once the entrails began to decompose, so did the wart. Chilblain sufferers stuck their fingers and toes inside a hot boiled turnip! Henna removed the dampness and odour from hands and feet and kept them dry and fragrant. Yoghurt was used for curing stomach upsets, and water-melon for reducing fever in typhoid.

There were three sorts of months, two sorts of hours and two categories of seasons.

No decision was ever made without consulting the stars or, on a lighter level, the Divan of Hafiz.

While all misfortune was blamed on Fate, cleverness was not admired; neither was the accumulation of wealth nor even the striving for independence.

Nothing was entirely total or irrevocable. Trespassing, in the territorial sense, had no meaning. The fish of the river and the fowls of the air belonged to anyone with enough wit to catch them.

The poorest of peasants felt obliged to leave some heads of wheat for the *Khushe-Chin* - this was a gypsy-like, nomadic character who was too poor and too feckless to cultivate and ended up by gleaning after the harvest.

Offences were dealt with personally. A child who stole, received a box on the ear, and an adult, a taste of the whip. Only enormities received police attention. Generally, people found the absence of law cheaper and less irksome.

Although the rule of the monarch was absolute, and his displeasure much feared, men did not always obey him blindly. There is the case of Prime Minister Sepahdar, who got into his carriage after an acrimonious interview with the Shah. On being asked by the coachman where he wanted to go, he replied, "To Europe," and to Europe they drove. Another politician, an ambassador in a European capital, on being informed that he was dismissed, observed, "The Embassy goes, but I stay." It turned out that his own mansion had been used as an embassy, free of rent, for so long that the fact of its ownership had been forgotten.

On the whole, a man who lived a good life and did not transgress, was considered fortunate.

As for a woman, her chastity was the most highly prized virtue. Once she ignored this she could be chased out of the community like a diseased dog.

***

Granny's young maid, Belghais, was over-developed and was showing a marked preference for male company. She had been chased away from the men-servants' quarters several times. One day, she declared that she was in love with the steward and wished to marry him. Before any decision could be made about this, she had climbed on the flat roof one afternoon, when the older people were asleep, and had undressed completely, exposing herself to all and sundry.

This so shocked my mother that she dismissed the girl at once. The matter was not so simple however, because her mother, Zahra, was a deaf mute and could not be separated from the girl. If they left, they would have nowhere to go and there would be no refuge. Zahra was in complete ignorance of the situation and was in great distress at the sudden upheaval. The only person who could have explained what had happened to her was her daughter, but she refused to do so. Mama was in a dilemma. She did not want the poor woman to be thrown out, and yet she could not keep the girl any longer. The steward was summoned and asked if he wished to take Belghais as a second wife. He said he might have considered the possibility before the girl had proved how unchaste she was. However, it was obvious to everyone that he did not want the deaf-mute for a mother-in-law. Eventually my mother's conscience was quietened by giving a sum of money to the women and asking the gardener to find them another position.

A similar solution was found when our favourite terriers, Terme and Meshki, were taken ill. These beautiful creatures were given to one of my brothers by a French family who were return-ing to France. We were asked to look after them particularly well and keep them warm as they were short-haired.

At first it was thought that they only responded to French. Soon, however, it was plain that they understood everything. Although bred in the city, they enjoyed country life with us in Meshkin-Abad. During cold weather, they slept under my parent's beds. In the morning, when they wished to be let out, they knocked their tails gently on the bottom of the bed, but never before some-one was awake.

One late spring, they both contracted distemper. It looked as though they would die. Apart from the fear of contagion, it was considered unlucky for any creature to die in the house. The dogs were taken to the ruins beyond the old city moat and left there with three days' food.

After a month, Terme, the bitch, turned up alone, having walked the four miles or so from where she had been left. She wagged her tail and was very pleased to be back.

Chapter 37

DIVERSIONS

I liked weddings as much for the feasts themselves as for the anti-cipation they aroused. Also they were the only times we heard gay music played by live musicians and watched dancing.

No sooner was a proposal made and accepted (through the parents of both sides) than an early date was fixed and preparations started. Invitation was either by word of mouth or, later, by card. One never received more than a week or ten days notice. The parents would go berserk, have their houses redecorated, their carpets washed, and chairs, tables and china hired. The dressmaker and the tailor worked their fingers to the bone and the gardener put geraniums and pansies in the borders.

Just as the last lucky month, before the two deadly unlucky ones approached, those who were contemplating marriage rushed into it just as though they were trying to qualify for tax relief.

As soon as the first wedding of the year was announced, my mother would get identical frilly dresses made for me and my sisters from some light material such as *crêpe de Chine* or chiffon, and they had to do for all the weddings for the rest of the year, regardless of the weather. We also had new European-imported shoes, which we bought from Geeve in Avenue Lalezar. It was a lovely shop and the leather smelt delicious.

Visits to the shops and dressmakers were often made in schooltime, which was good, and on the morning of the wedding we were dressed in our pretty clothes and sent to school so as to save time. We received much admiration from our friends who wanted to stand next to us in line. Of course, they did exactly the same to other girls when they came to school dressed for parties.

At the wedding, my mother usually sat with her friends and my sisters and I would be asked to sit in a row from which we could have a good view of the bride when she entered. We had instructions not to accept more than one glass of sherbet and not to stretch for sweetmeats. It was a bit boring sitting on those hard chairs for up to three hours, and we were glad that the wedding feasts no longer lasted for seven days, but there were quite a lot of diversions such as seeing complete strangers and noticing fashions and hair-dos free of the hated chador.

In those days, the religious ceremony was taken very seriously. The marriage prayer and contract was read aloud by a mullah from an adjoining chamber and listened to in silence. No widow or spinster was allowed in the bride's room. When the bride was asked for her consent, custom required that she pretend to deafness for the first two times and only gave her consent, in a quiet voice, at the third reading. As soon as this was done, pandemonium broke loose. Everyone cheered. Some threw small white sweets called *noghle* mixed with small golden coins over the bride's head and musicians burst into song. The bride and groom were taken into the reception room or in summer, to the garden and seated on stiff-backed chairs. Relatives would go forward to kiss and congratulate them and hand them precious presents. After a decent interval, the groom would cleverly find an opportunity to slip out and leave the bride on the hard seat for the remainder of the feast. The reception for male and female guests were held in separate halls or gardens, but female musicians and dancers entertained them both.

There was one occasion when we arrived for a wedding too early, at about three o'clock instead of five. It was a hot summer's day and we were surprised by the early invitation. When we got to the house, we discovered the messenger had made a mistake and so we offered to go back, but were pressed to go in. We were led into the garden, where two children were splashing water over the brick pavement, which was still hot. The plane trees against the high walls of the garden and those in the centre cast a welcome shadow and moved in a faint breeze. Chairs stacked on the backs of porters were pouring into the garden. Other *nammals* were bringing in the *khonche*, which is a very large flat loaf covered with the painted and gilded seeds of wild rue, arranged in pretty patterns and holy words. There were also two white and pink bowls made entirely of crystallized sugar in an exquisite lace pattern called *Kase Nabat* A large silver framed mirror and a copy of the Koran in a green leather binding were the groom's traditional present to the bride. Small trays of late apricots, early peaches and other fruit were carefully arranged in an almost perfect cone. Sweetmeats, small disc-shaped biscuits, various types of sweet and salted nuts were faultlessly arranged on fruit stands.

After offering us sherbets and asking us to make ourselves at home, our hostess excused herself saying, laughingly, that she was still busy bargaining with the groom about her daughter's settlement.

124

In Persia the bridegroom provides the bride with her jewellery and wedding clothes, pays for the wedding feast, and guarantees her an adequate sum, according to her station, should the marriage fail. On the other hand, the dowry, in the form of the household goods and furniture that the bride's parents provide, is not obligatory although it is a matter of face, and is usually of equal value to the groom's wedding expenses.

We roamed about. In a small back room an old woman was smoking opium and a child's hair was being washed against her will. Mama asked where we could see the bride. The old woman took the pipe out of her mouth and said, "Go to the second courtyard on the right."

We found the bride in the process of being beautified. Her hair was being curled with a pair of curling tongs heated over a charcoal brazier, her face pasted with some white stuff called *sefid-ab*, and some Persian rouge. Mama congratulated her and wished her well. She did not reply. Brides were traditionally modest and taciturn.

On returning to the garden where time stood still but the shadows of the plane trees did not, I suddenly felt that no matter what happened to the rest of the day or to the lives of this shy bride and her unseen groom, I would never forget the charm of that afternoon when everything seemed good, natural and unspoilt.

***

A funeral could also be an enjoyable occasion, provided it was not that of a breadwinner or a young and happy person. It was often difficult to tell genuine grief from the formal expression of mourning, which was compulsory for any bereaved person. The burial of the deceased is a matter of great urgency in Islamic law, and the dead are buried in the presence of next of kin as soon as possible. What is called a funeral is really the service which used to be held for three consecutive days in the family home or a mosque a few days after the burial. The bereaved, dressed all in black with a black veil, would sit at the top of the room. Relatives and friends, also in black and with long faces, would call in relays. At the sight of each new arrival the bereaved would wail, and the visitor would utter some word of condolence and then take a seat against the wall and be served with most delicious black coffee in a tiny cup.

In the centre of the room, a large cashmere shawl would be spread and three large Chinese jars placed on it, as well as a number of beautifully bound Korans and prayer books. Apart from these, the only other props were three or four sinister and hard looking middle-aged women, in cheap, black clothes, the hired mourners who chanted and wailed every time the hostess' strength failed. The whole outfit was hired from a famous woman mourner called Mohtaram-el-Zakerine, whose mother had been an entertainer and later turned respectable. She supervised the affair personally and led the chanting.

You were expected to leave as soon as you had done your duty and had drunk your scented coffee. Alas, not if you were a close relative such as a niece or a cousin. In that case you sat for three whole days and the performance was repeated on the eve of the seventh day, the fortieth day and the first anniversary. After the first morning, you got numb with boredom, but excellent meals were cooked and served on these occasions and if you were lucky you could, sometimes, witness the height of bad manners and sheer exhibitionism displayed by friends and relatives. There was the time when a woman attending her sister's funeral, whom she had constantly refused to help during her lifetime, stretched herself between the amphorae and lay there for an hour for all to see before she got up and ate a hearty meal. Later when her mother died at the age of 108 she arrived at the funeral in a towering rage and publicly accused her sister-in-law, who had been looking after the deceased for half a century, of having strangled her.

These things happened sometimes, but there was also a lot of genuine grief at death, and not many instances of pleasure at the impending legacy. This was either because Persians being poor there was not much to go round, or because having suffered instability throughout their long history they had learned not to value worldly possessions.

***

As previously mentioned, in Persia we observe two different calendars: the solar year, beginning with the Vernal equinox on

21st March, which is celebrated by the festival of *Noruz*, and a calendar based on a lunar calculation, which is a purely Moslem system, widespread in the Mohammedan world. Although the starting point for both systems is the year of the *Hejirat* (the Prophet Mohamad's flight from Mecca to Medina in the year 622 a.d.) the lunar year is shorter by some ten days. As a result of this, although all the important occasions in the solar year (e.g. the festival of *Noruz*) have a fixed date, the events of the lunar year rotate crazily round the seasons and clash with the solar fixtures. I remember *Ramadan* coinciding with *Noruz* which meant you could neither eat nor drink during the days of the festival for three years running. Even worse, when *Moharam* fell on *Noruz* it meant farewell to all celebrations for six years. Imagine, if you can, although it is a ridiculous analogy, Good Friday falling on the same day as Christmas.

The lunar year has several holy days, practically all of them mournful occasions. The month of *Ramadan*, which gradually moves from mid-winter to mid-summer, is, in spite of the feasting, a happy occasion in the Sunni world. But it is marred for the Shia sect by the martyrdom of the beloved Imam Ali in the third week of *Ramadan*. His death was a great blow to the aspirations of the Shias, and it has been commemorated ever since by three days of mourning. Then there are the two tragic months of *Moharam* and *Safar* during which the Imams Hassan and Hossain and their followers were martyred. These are two, dismal, gloomy months during which no celebration can take place or pleasures allowed.

When I first became conscious of days and months, *Ramadan* arrived in winter when days were short, and so was the ordeal of the True Believer. You were awakened before sunrise by the sound of a cannon, ate a huge meal in a hurry, kept thirsty all day, slept all afternoon and woke with the sound of another cannon at sunset to announce that you might now break your fast. People became lethargic and aloof, and their breath became nasty towards the end of the day. Only children, the very old and infirm were exempt. In some families where the masters did not fast, it was harder on the servants who had to prepare meals on empty stomachs. As fasting was one of the tenets of Islam and the non-observance of it sinful, one could not eat or drink in public, nor smoke. Consequently there was a lot of hypocrisy. Many men had to rush back to the privacy of their homes for a meal or a drink.

At the end of *Ramadan* came the feast of *Fetre*, an occasion for over-indulgence and rejoicing. On that day, you gave to the needy the equivalent value of the amount of money saved on food by fasting during *Ramadan*. My father used to double the alms to absolve us all.

I never discovered the extent of my father's religious convictions. Once, during a sickness when I nursed him, before he fell asleep he quietly murmured his *Ash-had*, a prayer similar to the twenty-third Psalm. I asked Mama if he expected to die that night. She said that this was his only regular daily prayer.

At the beginning of *Moharam* (which then occurred about the middle of Spring) all normal activities ceased. One went into deep mourning and dressed in black from head to toe. Everywhere there was *Roze*. Processions roamed the streets carrying black standards. Men beat themselves with chains, cutting the skin of their breasts and foreheads, simulating the great tragedy of Karbela. Some wore shrouds covered in fresh blood, and chanted "Hassan! Hossain!" which alluded to the martyred saints of the Shia sect.

Everywhere meals were prepared and the poor fed. A charming passion play, called *Taazieh*, was put on and the atmosphere became very tense as you neared the date of the martyrdoms. You had to pretend to feel grief all the time. If so much as the sound of a gramophone was heard from your house you ran the risk of being branded a heretic and mobbed.

For a child who could not understand the national and historical need for separateness, this seemed altogether too excessive and too long.

***

Dressed in black rep dresses and wrapped in black rep *chadors*, we trudged our way back from school. It was hot and the attendance had been cut to mornings only, since the middle of May.

We now favoured the alternative route, the tree-lined Avenue Ghavam-Saltaneh. It was shady and on both sides there were *joubs* or small water channels. This was an elegant street with large gardens and huge gates on either side. One of these mansions was then the property of the famous Prime Minister, Ghavam-e-Saltaneh and rented by the Egyptian Embassy. Then came a terrace of two storey houses with handsome balconies. On the ground floor, one could often see old women, and smell fried onions. On the balconies stood enviable young Armenian girls in coloured dresses, talking and laughing.

We had given up the game of touching doors. Instead we were jumping across the *joub* and back again in between the trees. Further along we had the choice of three roads to take us to Yousef-Abad and home. In one of these roads we passed a door behind which a dog was always whining and sometimes yelping as though in pain. Once the door of the garden was ajar and we saw a greyhound tied to a post and left in the sun without water. He was panting desperately and we felt very sorry for it. From that time on, we avoided that road and this left the three of us only two choices and much argument ensued. The orderly who was escorting us wanted to know why we had abandoned our former routine of choosing a road a day in turn.

"It is that wretched dog. He howls so much."

"That is because his master has gone to Rasht and Hassan doesn't want the dog to run away. He keeps it chained all day."

"Who is Hassan?"

"He's the servant. I meet him at the baker's."

"Well, tell him that the dog will get rabies if he is kept in the sun. Then it will bite him and he'll go mad."

"He also says that the dog is dirty. He makes a mess where he is tied up and no amount of beating will help."

"The poor thing has no choice, has he? Tell him to tie a rope round his neck and take him into the street."

Whether or not Hassan was sufficiently frightened into treating the animal humanely, we do not know. We only hoped that, once untied, the dog had the sense to escape from that miserable house - as we ourselves escaped from the miserable city.

Chapter 38

RENEWAL

Once in Meshkin-Abad, we discarded the ugly *chador*, the black dress and the hypocritical expression of grief. Everyone seemed hopeful and happy here. The peasants were too sensible to indulge in that sort of nonsense. The crops were ripening and the early fruit already picked. The land exuded warmth and richness.

After greeting our four-legged friends and revisiting the spots we loved, we settled into a routine of near bliss. In the morning we had to help Mama in whatever she was doing: embroidering yards of velvet mantlepiece covers, or reading obscure poetry books. At noon, everything stopped. The chatter of the cicadas stood out in the hot silence. We had a cool lunch, usually based on rice, yogurt and fruit and then we slept. At four o'clock we gathered on the east verandah to take tea or melon and waited for an hour before it got cool enough to go for our walk. If we delayed this, Zanbouz barked impatiently and shook his yellow mane.

It is difficult now to remember what we talked about while we were walking. It was probably about who was likely to visit us that summer, our friends at school, our brothers and the future. All the time we were conscious of the sky which by now had a few specks of cloud in the west. They looked like piles of gauze, or copper dishes flattened out and extended. We jumped over ditches and cut our bare legs on camel thorn. Zanbouz dug for rodents and chased birds. Sometimes, too fast for reality, Jamshid's bicycle appeared and disappeared. All the time we watched for the great climax of the day, the setting of the sun. It was magnificent.

A slight breeze disturbed the air and the temperature dropped. The flocks and herds returned from grazing, making much noise and dust. After much braying and mooing and bleating they were milked, fed and settled for the night. The young made little satisfied noises and then there was silence. The water-birds stuck

their heads under their wings, made a sound as though of acknow-
ledgement (we called this 'prayer') and slept. Men walked home
with spades on their shoulders and bundles in their hands.

We sat on the faded canvas chairs in the drive looking at the
bright stars and arguing how we could rearrange them in pretty
patterns. The dogs had begun their nightly vigil and the mosquitoes sucked our blood. We wrapped our long skirts tighter and
tighter round our legs, but they still bit.

Someone brought out a hurricane lamp. We fetched the old
hand-wound gramophone and our meagre collection of records.
Papa's favourite singer, Chaliapin, Nosrat's great love, the *Kreutzer
Sonata* played by the boy Menuhin - his picture on the cover almost rubbed off with kisses - Brahm's *Hungarian Dances*, also one
or two Persian and Turkish records.

As we sat listening to these, the darkness thickened. We could
hear our parents talking and drinking close by, but could not see
them. Shadows moved in the dark. Peasant women attracted by
the sound of music drifted towards it and sat at a distance on the
gravel. We started with Beethoven. The young Menuhin had moved
from *Adagio Sostenuto* to *Andante*. As variation followed variation, I became aware of a sense of common identity. Dogs, women,
children and we ourselves fused into one. The sweet, melancholic
dialogue of the violin and the piano affected us equally and the
slow plucking of the strings plucked at all our hearts. We had all
fallen under the spell and there was not a sound. Even the babies,
tied uncomfortably on their mother's backs, did not move. If
music had such a uniting effect, I wondered, why was it so persistently denied us by our religion? Surely it could do more good than
harm.

I think the women thought that a gramophone was a form of
music box which made and emitted all the sounds, but when we
came to the singing of Chaliapin, they got rather puzzled. When
the record stopped, they asked if a little man was trapped inside
the box. We told them that only his voice was trapped. They were
even more puzzled.

As soon as the concert came to an end, the women got up
and left as they had come, silently without saying a word. These
occasions moved me greatly. Who would have thought Persian
peasants would have liked listening to Beethoven?

131

Between eight and nine we had dinner, indoors, by the light of a squat oil lamp, and went to bed soon after. Beds were made of old planks, inexpertly joined together by the village carpenter, and were incredibly hard. To each corner was attached a post and on these a rectangular tent of a mosquito-net erected. The beds were in the open air in a crescent in front of the house.

I did not sleep immediately, but listened for the bells of the camel caravan which passed the water-mill each night, less than a mile away. There were no railways yet and only a few lorries. Nine-tenths of all goods and passengers moved on mules and camel-back. The first few camels in the caravan had on their necks, bells of different sizes and tones in consecutive order, and the even, slow movement of the camels' gait rang these in a most charming manner. For years I was at a loss to describe the sound, until a few years ago, a friend introduced me to Bach's *Concerto for Violin Oboe and String Orchestra in D Minor*. We played the first movement and reached the *adagio* and there it was, camels' gait, bells swaying, and all in the form of the slow, even response of the harpsichord.

The camelteer, to keep himself awake, sang poems of Hafiz and Ferdosi. His diction and music were faultless, and you wondered with that voice, what he was doing among camels in the midst of the night?

"The fear of tide, a whirlpool so perilous and the black night.
How can the light-hearted shore dweller know our plight?"
(Hafiz)

I remembered my father's story of an ancient Persian musician who, because he was being persecuted, appeared in disguise among his enemies and produced such gay music that everyone hopped about and danced. Then he switched to sad music. His listeners were overcome by grief and fainted. He slipped out of the feast and joining a caravan he rearranged the bells on the camels' necks. This stimulated the animals and in the morning it was found that instead of the usual ten miles, they had travelled over twenty and were well out of the enemy's reach. Is anyone ever out of the enemy's reach I wondered.

"The fear of tide, a whirlpool so perilous and the black night.
How can the light-hearted shore dweller know our plight?"

How indeed? How can one know the plight of a bush or a
tree? These peasants were so passive and inarticulate. Time had no
meaning whatsoever here. If they needed something they would
come to the gate and pull the rope which rang the large bronze
bell. Whether they wished to borrow a tool, or whether a child
was dying, they did not ring twice. Someone walked slowly to the
gate and received the message. He either delivered it or forgot it. It
never occurred to the supplicant to press his case. He crouched on
the gravel and waited for someone to pass by before he took his
second chance. If the response was slow or did not come, he never
got angry or annoyed.

His needs were elementary, so were his cares. I remember
years ago we were invited to Soghra's wedding. Mama did not
come, but sent us along with the women servants. Soghra's father
was an elder of the village and provided generously for the feast.
He had a couple of sheep slaughtered and a lot of rice cooked.
Two men played the drum and some youths danced. The servants
were scornful about the quality of cooking and music. At their
suggestion, my mother sent the bride a length of silk to cover her
hair, otherwise the girl would have been hidden by a coarse, red
cloth, which is the peasant's colour for joy.

The house stank of cow-dung and the peasants were gathered
in their only, everyday clothes. In spite of our servants' scorn, the
company were as happy as at any other wedding party. What was
it that made them so happy amidst such poverty? Perhaps it was
their extreme innocence, the lack of care and responsibility. My
mother or Fateme-Baji, our housekeeper, always moved about
with a large bunch of keys. These people had no need of keys.
Nothing to lock up, no wedding or funeral clothes. No decoration
on their cake, in fact, no cake at all. Their greatest dream was to
visit one of the minor, holy shrines hung with gaudy mirrors and
damask. Though they did not expect to plan this. If it happened,
it made them supremely happy. I now wondered whether that gift
of a silk veil was such a good idea after all? Every action must have
a consequence.

Suppose we gave these people a lot more; gave them all we possessed including all our cares and consciousness, would it increase their happiness?

Like the pear tree in our garden or the walnut tree near the back of the *ghaleh*, these people bore their fruits, and dropped them on the soil to become organic matter, and not a single one was picked to grace a king's table. The first place they knew at birth was a mud-brick on which a peasant's confinement took place. (A Persian peasant traditionally gave birth on a mud brick). Sooner or later a mud brick was all that was left of him in the form of a headstone.

A shooting star darted through the northern sky, followed immediately by another. These, someone had said, represented souls that had just departed. The sky was still full of stars.

Chapter 39

MISHKA AND THE FRENCH PROFESSOR

Before the advent of the airliner, travelling was thought to be dangerous and undesirable and those who went away on long journeys were considered as good as lost. It was therefore with great relief and rejoicing that my relatives received the return of their young men after they had completed their education in Europe. These young, spirited men had given up the horse for the more adventurous aeroplane. Two of them had qualified as pilots in Kharkov and had come back with amazing stories of life in Soviet Russia. An older cousin Ahmad Khan Nakhjavan was the first member of our family to go in for flying. He had been educated in France and returned to Persia with a promising future. Another cousin went as far as becoming a naval officer, having been trained in Italy. Everyone wondered where he would sail. The southern Persian ports were collectively hellish and uninhabitable. The Caspian Sea was separated from the rest of the country by the Albourz range which had not yet been tunnelled. So it was jokingly suggested that he would sail on the Karaj river, at times hardly bigger than a stream. And thus it was that Bishana's rooms became thronged with handsome young men and their proud parents who had come to pay her homage. And Bishana, like Queen Victoria, played a universal grandmother.

About this time we had two other visitors, both strangers and unexpected. One morning, a young European gentleman presented himself at the door. He had been Nosrat's music teacher in France and had come to stay at my brother's invitation, which had been issued a long time ago. His name was Monsieur Proove. He had taught Nosrat the violin and they had talked about the quality of life in Persia. Nosrat, as expected, had said, "It is a wonderful life; why don't you come and see for yourself?" So he had come, leaving his wife and son behind. He stayed for eighteen months.

The evening of the same day, an army lorry stopped outside our door and unloaded what appeared to be a large mountain bear. All the information the driver could give was that it belonged to Captain Safar-Ali Khan and it had been sent from Parchin "to recuperate". There was nothing for it but to take it by its chain and leave it in the stables for the moment.

My brother Ali, still in his mountain garrison, was surrounding himself with clowns and wild animals. Mama rang him and found out that his pet was a lady bear called Mishka, who had been captured as a cub in the mountains and sold to him. She had been well behaved and popular with the garrison. On her daily round, she extracted a loaf of bread from the bakers, fruit and a bottle of beer from the "shop". One day some youngsters had replaced the beer with petrol, which had nearly killed poor Mishka. Thus the need for a change. Asked about his future plans for the bear, he had been vague and had suggested that she would be happy in the stables.

Monsieur Proove was stabled in the guests' villa with my two brothers. Unlike the bear, he was clean, quiet and undemanding, much more like a well-bred young Englishman than a Frenchman. His presence was generally welcomed. He spoke French with my brothers and kept them happy with his music. He was particularly kind to our dogs and to Mishka. For her part, the bear adored him,

135

rubbed her chin on his feet and rolled on her back like a dog at his approach.

One day my brothers were having tea in the garden and the Frenchman was playing the violin. The stable doors were left open and the bear walked into the garden upsetting the tea-things and tried to hug him. Then she went a bit wild and climbed a mulberry tree.

She had been taught by her keeper to pretend to smoke an unlit cigarette and to imitate the sound of a motor by blowing with her mouth through her toes. She was an engaging creature. As her strength returned, she exercised her lungs by letting out a most fearsome yell several times a day.

Both the musician and the bear were immensely liked by our friends and relatives who insisted on seeing them when they called, and invited Proove out with my brothers.

I remember a family luncheon in our house to celebrate my cousins' safe return from Europe. Everyone was there and the place was like Bedlam. Children were giggling, men drinking and women chattering. Proove, standing up valiantly to all this, was dutifully playing a violin sonata punctuated by Mishka's ear-splitting yells.

One night Proove was asked out to a birthday party. He returned home in the early hours so ill that he had to be rushed into hospital. Fortunately it turned out to be an excess of wind and fish but this incident gave my family a shock and they decided that in the prevailing political atmosphere it would be damaging to have a foreigner die on your hands. So he was found lodgings with an Armenian family in the same *kuche*. But he spent most of his time in the villa. Later he was found a job as *nazim* (or superintendant) in the Franco-Persian Boys' School which my two younger brothers attended. His job was to keep the boys in order, which he was not very good at, and to ring a hand-bell which the boys said sarcastically, he did beautifully "having for some time been Motreb (entertainer) to the house of Ansari."

The other main attraction, Mishka, had become loud and restless, and was also disposed of. She was sent to Meshkin-Abad tied in a strong sack and loaded on the back of a mule whom she bit several times, and who bolted, dropping her, sack and all.

Her fate seemed a bit unfair compared with that of the *Kher-seh*, another Persian mountain bear, who for the crime of frightening nannies at the British Embassy compound in Gholak, was ceremoniously put on the plane returning to Europe which had just brought Mr. Churchill to the Tehran conference. He was placed in the London Zoo where he entertained countless visitors for years to come.

Chapter 40

THE BED

My tummy-ache was blamed on the water-melon. I had been greedy and eaten too much.

In fact I had not over indulged. It was the end of the summer when water-melons lose their scent and acquire a mushy taste. I was told to go and lie down until the pain went. It was early afternoon. I remember lying on a rug on the western verandah trying to get some warmth from the low sun, but a cool wind was preventing this. Around me people were bustling, loading things into the Ford. We were leaving for the city that afternoon and the term would start shortly. I felt shivery and light-headed as I squeezed myself among the bodies and the luggage. Every road bump brought on a fresh wave of pain. It was an interminable journey.

When we got to Tehran we found that our uncle Mirpanj with my aunt and their eight children and servants had arrived from Ghazvin and were going to stay with us. What was more, they expected visitors that night. Weary and unprepared as we were, this caused a mild shock. At least twelve extra beds had to be made. All the chickens that we had brought from the village had to be plucked and cooked. Rice, vegetables, pickles, and sweets got ready. In short, a fair-sized feast prepared at three hours' notice. Naturally everyone got working frenziedly and nobody had an ear for my pain.

Between two large rooms, one of which was a reception and the other, an improvised dining-room, was a small room with various uses, of which one was a passage. It had a garden door facing north and three other doors. In one corner, for some reason, there was a single metal bedstead and a mattress. Sometimes young men sat on it and smoked a cigarette. At other times children used the springs as a trampoline.

I crept under this bed, tried to get myself into a comfortable position and fell asleep. I woke up feeling cold. Sounds of chatter came from the reception room. A man's voice trying to be heard, laughter, then more chatter. It all sounded far away and I felt no desire to join the party.

Inside myself, strange things were happening. I felt that, like a log cracked under an axe, my being had been split into chunks. One was lying there with inertia, vaguely aware of external sensations. Another part of me was busy delving into the past; and, as if by magic, veil after veil were lifting from the years of my childhood. Like shots from a film, I saw scenes of pleasure, serenity and distress pass before my eyes. Names that I had forgotten long ago came back like a roll-call. Events flashed across my mind with an amazing clarity and their meaning explained. Identities kept changing. I was myself and also other people and animals. I recollected the time I had pinched my younger sister's cheek for upsetting our lunch on the pavement at school. But in this instance, I was not only myself inflicting the pain, but I was also Maryam receiving it.

I was aware of the servants bringing trays of food through the garden door and two of my girl cousins laying the dishes on the cloth. The door was left open and a gale blew over me. I shivered. Now I was the donkey on whose back ice was loaded all day long. Now and again its shoulders shuddered, but it was not able to complain. Azra had said that its back was covered in sores.

A khaki coat was hanging on the edge of the bed. I pulled it down over me. That was better, but I could not stop the backward journey of my memory, nor the turmoil of my mind. What will happen when I reach the source, my mother's womb? Will there be a final revelation and death? Rhymes kept beating in my temple:

"Seeing the scythe of the new moon and the field of the sky
    so deep,

I was reminded of my own cultivation and the time to reap.
I cried 'O Fortune thou slept and now the sun has risen,'
He replied 'Non-the-less do not despair of the past.
Should'st thou go to Heaven, Christ-like, good and innocent,
    we are told,
From thy radiance the sun will be enriched a thousand
    fold.'"

The chatter which had stopped resumed, but it sounded very close, as though two people were sitting on the bed. One unfamiliar voice said, "The rice was quite inedible. It tasted smokey." Another voice replied, "But wasn't it funny that fat maid upsetting the *Khoresht* on the cloth. Their servants aren't very skilled, are they?"

While I listened to this with one ear the other was listening to a more congenial voice declaiming:

"These aspiring seekers of Him are unaware,
    Those who know, alas, can not declare!"

How could *I* declare? Would anyone understand if I told them? Told what? That I became somebody else? A deaf mute who could only weep when her world collapsed? A dog tied all day under a fierce sun and beaten? Would they understand me any better than they could understand that dog?

The storm in my brain became a whirlwind. I was blown over the clouds into a bleak desert; the sort of place where saints were martyred. But instead of warriors and camels there was an army of deserted women holding small children by the hand. Men with huge scrotums dragging their painful bodies about and mangy dogs and donkeys panting and suffering. A mullah on a rotating pulpit was insisting that: *"Ensan Ashrafe Makhlughat Ast."* (Man is God's noblest creature."

The past, present and future all got rolled into one and fragments of it blew about like ashes of burnt paper. Everything seemed to whirl around and carry me along, hypnotised and numb.

A cool hand touched my leg. It was Azra. She whispered, "There you are. I have been looking everywhere for you."

139

I peeped out of my corner. Daylight poured in through the fanlight. I saw a pair of moustaches going up and down to the accompaniment of a gentle snore. My uncle Mirpange had been allocated the bed. It seemed incredible that I was still alive after all that I had been through and that my pain was getting better.

"I must tell you something," I said, trying to put my extraordinary adventure into words.

"I had noticed," said Azra shortly. While she helped me wash and clean up she said, "You have become an adult. From now on you must behave like one. It is childish to play truant like that."

I said, "I believe the dinner was a disaster. What went wrong?"

"So you were awake all the time and you didn't show up. Did you know that one of the visitors had to go home in a borrowed overcoat as he couldn't find his own and the servants were suspected of stealing it? I see you had it all the time. I'd better tell your Mama."

"Oh, please don't," I pleaded.

As she served me with a breakfast of tea, fresh bread, dried cream and honey, I got stronger and the memories of the previous night's experience receded. I tried desperately to hang onto them.

"Do you remember," I asked, "the time, many summers ago, when we hired a house in Shemiran? Every afternoon we went picnicking with you or Abji in the countryside. One day as we were eating our bread and thick yogurt, on a rock in a gorge, two men servants suddenly rushed from home to warn us that there was about to be a flood. They picked me up but Zari refused to be carried, saying that the men smelt of cooking. When we got out of the gorge, we saw a thick, brown mud sweeping through the valley. Do you remember it?"

"Yes. What of it?"

"I saw it all again last night," I said feebly.

"There you go again," she said sternly. "You must stop this childishness. Do you know who usurped your bed last night?"

"No."

"One of your boy cousins and if you are not smart tonight you will lose it again. He will sleep in it as by right and you would have to creep under Mirpange's bed."

140

Like Terme and Meshki, I thought wistfully.

When the implication of her warning sank in I realised that she was right. I must wake up and join the household in their passive and subtle resistance against the invading relatives.

There is a Persian saying, "A guest is friend of God." One might well add "only".

Later that week, my very devout aunt came to stay. I was summoned to her presence and taken to task about my religious observances. Had I ever fasted for a whole week, let alone a month, she wanted to know. Had I ever prayed regularly? The answer was, of course, no.

Then carefully and patiently she explained all the tenets of Islam and all the laws concerning ablution, fasting and prayer; then she said, "Up to now you have been free of obligation because our kind religion regards children as sinless till they reach puberty. Now you are entirely responsible for your own actions. Not only are you answerable for your bad deeds, but also for the lack of good ones. From now on you must pray five times a day, fast throughout *Ramadan*, and keep your face covered from all men outside your family."

I felt very perplexed. Problems were being piled on my head. Not that I envisaged myself doing anything exactly wicked, but it seemed that omission was as bad as commission. The paralysingly dull routine of prayer and fasting would kill me. In any case how could I keep a day's fast passing through an orchard full of ripe nectarines? or not interrupt my prayers with laughter if Jamshid insisted on making funny remarks? As for keeping chaste by covering myself in an ugly *chador*, voluntarily, for the rest of my life, I disagreed with it most strongly and had no intention of complying if I had a choice, but I could not say so.

Just when I thought the dreaded interview was over, and I was preparing to take my leave, my aunt said something really alarming.

"You are thirteen now and no doubt soon you will be given in marriage and have children. You must prepare yourself for the moral responsibility of a wife and mother."

Good God! I married? What a terrible suggestion! It was bad enough to be expelled from the green pastures of innocence, to be made to pray and fast and behave like an old woman, but to be "given in marriage soon" - that was preposterous. I felt like a habitual gambler who is suddenly not only made to face his debts, but made responsible for other gamblers. The prospect was terrifying, still there was nothing I could do but say what all true Persians say in times of peril *"Khoda Bozorge"* - God is great. He will find a way.